Care of Older People

This text provides a foundation of essential knowledge and practical guidance for building best practice in the care of older people.

Fully updated for its second edition, *Care of Older People* uses a whole-person and values-led approach to explore practice with older people, providing the opportunity for practitioners to reflect critically on not just *what* they do but also on *how* and *why*. It includes two new chapters, the first looking at the ways in which digital technologies can impact on how care support is delivered and the potential for older people's lives to be enriched or otherwise by them, and the second reflecting the particular challenges of helping older people at the end of their lives to manage their needs. Highlighting how older people in receipt of care support can be enabled to be co-producers of knowledge, it challenges the depiction of older people with support needs as one-dimensional individuals rather than multi-dimensional people with life left to live.

This accessible book is an invaluable learning resource for all those working, or studying, across the caring professions, including social work, social care, nursing, occupational therapy and anyone committed to excellence in eldercare.

Dr Sue Thompson has many years' experience as a nurse, social worker, care manager, practice teacher, distance learning tutor, researcher and writer of working in the field of eldercare. Throughout her career, her passion has been to promote eldercare practice which is driven by a desire on the part of those who support dependent older people to help them to live, as far as is possible, the life they want to be living.

'This manual has long been needed. The care of older people is not only an important topic, but has been a neglected area, both practically and academically. Sue Thompson has produced a compassionate, conceptually sophisticated, and extremely practical approach to eldercare. Her knowledge of the field, conceptual thinking and practical understanding will make this book invaluable for caregivers. It is a must read, a gift to all who will read it. Exceptionally well written, it is filled with stories, practical suggestions, and conceptual backing for the ideas presented. The book offers fresh hope and comfort to those making the journey of life.'

Dr Gerry R. Cox is *Professor Emeritus of Sociology at University of Wisconsin–La Crosse, USA*

'This is a long overdue manual which offers a first-class guide to working with elderly people. The concept that older people are people with problems and not the problem is central to the author's whole approach and is a refreshing change from so much of the literature. I especially like the fact students and workers can study at their own pace and in what order they like but supported by the centrality of reflective practice throughout. This latter element is particularly well designed, demanding that participants think through what are often complex and multi-dimensional issues surrounding eldercare. An excellent resource I heartily endorse.'

Dr John Bates, *former Head of Social Work & Social Justice, Liverpool Hope University*

Care of Older People

A Values Perspective

Second Edition

Sue Thompson

Routledge
Taylor & Francis Group

LONDON AND NEW YORK

Designed cover image: Getty Images

Second edition published 2026
by Routledge
4 Park Square, Milton Park, Abingdon, Oxon, OX14 4RN

and by Routledge
605 Third Avenue, New York, NY 10158

Routledge is an imprint of the Taylor & Francis Group, an informa business

First edition published 2018 by Avenue Media Solution

British Library Cataloguing-in-Publication Data
A catalogue record for this book is available from the British Library

ISBN: 9781041077916 (hbk)
ISBN: 9781916925908 (pbk)
ISBN: 9781041054481 (ebk)

DOI: 10.4324/9781041054481

Typeset in Times New Roman
by codeMantra

Contents

CONTENTS

Welcome

... to this manual on caring for older people. It has been put together to serve as a guide for those people who work on a daily basis or are training to do so, with older people who have become significantly dependent on others for help to get through each day. Practice that is not informed by values, policy, research, knowledge-sharing initiatives and so on has the potential to be ineffective or even dangerous and I cannot stress enough how important it is that we draw on the vast knowledge base that exists about eldercare to inform what we do. Thinking and doing are *both* important elements of our work and thinking about the relationship between the two is so important if we are to do what we do to the best of our abilities and with the best possible outcomes. Having said that, the main focus in this manual is on practice – informed practice, yes – but with an emphasis on doing, rather than theorising about doing, important though that is.

I have described it as a guide because it does indeed contain some guidance and food for thought about issues that I know are of concern to older people who need our support, and as a manual because you will bring your own 'hand' to it by reflecting on how this relates to your own workplace and work practices.

The intention has never been to offer easy answers because, in situations where we are working with people rather than things, then we cannot get away from the fact that we are immersed in life's complexities and so there won't be any easy answers. Working in eldercare can be fulfilling but it is not easy and, if we are committed to supporting those older people we work with to live fulfilling lives too, then we owe it to them to take, or create, whatever opportunities we can to help us to do the best job that we can. With that in mind, I hope you will enjoy reading through what follows and reflecting on how it relates to your own work and values.

Happy thinking!

About the author

Dr Sue Thompson has many years' experience as a nurse, social worker, care manager, practice teacher, distance learning tutor, researcher and writer of working in the field of eldercare. Throughout her career, her passion has been to promote eldercare practice which is driven by a desire on the part of those who support dependent older people to help them to live, as far as is possible, the life they want to be living. This passion inspired her PhD study on reciprocity in old age, where she explored whether a sense of 'usefulness' remains important to older people's self-esteem and spiritual well-being when they become significantly dependent on others, and whether this is recognised by those undertaking assessments of their care needs.

Foreword

For many years, ageism prevented books from being written on older people because of the intense interest in children by practitioners. This is not to deny the importance and significance of that group of people at one end of the life-course, but, historically, a focus on younger people has added to the marginality and invisibility of older people. Worse, because there were hardly any widely subscribed postgraduate courses in social work with older people due to the over-whelming focus on children, there were periodic episodes of inhumanity against older people (known today as 'elder abuse').

It was a forgotten dimension that older people were actually *people*. There was also a chronic shortage of research and knowledge for carers, families and the health and social work professions on the vulnerabilities of older people, whether they lived at home or in a care home. Peter Townsend wrote his dev-astating overview of 'care' in his famous book *The Last Refuge*, arguing that care homes were not necessarily benevolent institutions but 'warehouses' where care was in chaos, as carers did not have sufficient skills, knowledge and experi-ence to work appropriately with older people. Hence, while books on policy and theory in caring for older people are important, this practice manual by Dr Sue Thompson outshines them all. This is a magnificent piece of writing. The reason-ing is utterly compelling; the quality of the writing is not only fluid and critical, but also concise and littered with practice examples.

It does what no other practice manual does. What Sue Thompson has achieved is a tour de force in highlighting to carers and the health and care professions the implications of, and the opportunities involved in, caring with, caring for and caring about older people. The manual really excels, in that she cleverly highlights that there is no duality in terms of *thinking about* practice and *doing* practice. For a long time there was a demarcation in the study of old age between thinkers and doers. Estes and Minkler used to implicitly suggest there was some form of exaggerated age wars between thinkers and those who investigate older people's experiences (doers).

This manual deconstructs and smashes such assumptions and, with an intellectual wallop, synthesises the importance of thinking and doing for effective practice. I have rarely read a book that addresses this, and so this is one of the first in the world to go beyond the dualism that sets thinking and practice apart. They are two sides of the same coin, not in opposition. This is a masterclass in bringing the two together.

It is exceptionally well packaged, with concepts clearly explained, an extremely thoughtful style, as well as being beautifully well crafted and impeccably well structured. There are 12 sections, each written in a distinctive style. Those familiar with Sue Thompson's work will know her extraordinary ability to shed light on the importance of *valuing* older people.

This is one of those rare sources that gets the reader to engage from the beginning to the end and beyond. I say beyond because reading the manual can engage the reader to think deeply and focus on what it means to be cared for by a variety of people and professions. It is influential in getting the reader to transform their attitudes. She addresses social divisions head on and, in depth and breadth, she is extremely thoughtful in suggesting case studies where she highlights context-sensitive situations where people can learn from working with older people.

This manual has it all. I very strongly endorse it and would go so far as to say that it is one of the greatest books I have ever read on caring for older people and deserves to be widely cited globally.

Professor Jason L. Powell

Acknowledgements

I'll not name them individually but thank you to everyone at Taylor and Francis and also Critical Publishing who provided guidance and support in bringing this publication to fruition. Many thanks to Professor Jason Powell for providing the foreword, and by way of this, an endorsement of the value of my work. Thanks also to Dr John Bates and Dr Gerry Cox for their kind words of support. As always, I am indebted to Neil and Anna Thompson for their moral and technical support, not only during this project but in all of my endeavours. Last, but definitely not least, thanks are due to those older people who are recipients of care support and, by providing feedback on the quality of that support, are co-producers of the critical gerontology knowledge base which has informed my practice and writing.

Introduction

I hope you will find this manual useful and am confident that you will be repaid for the effort you make to work through it. It is divided into 12 chapters. I would like to have included many, many more, as the provision of and funding for eldercare is such a vast and diverse enterprise. According to the most recent census in 2021 (Office for National Statistics), approximately 18% of the population of England and Wales are aged 65 years or older (and mention is made that the situation in Scotland and Northern Ireland is likely to be similar) so we're talking about a lot of potentially dependent people here, especially given that 2.4% are aged over 85 years – the latter group containing those most likely to be suffering from the ill-health that can, though not necessarily does, accompany old age. Those percentages translate into there being over 11 million people over 65 and 1 1/2 million over 85. Furthermore, according to Age UK projections, the number is set to continue rising. Given that social care has been, and continues to be, underfunded and undervalued, then there is cause to be concerned about the quality of care that older people can expect to receive and for increasing workloads to put more and more pressure on already busy social care workers like yourself.

This state of affairs makes it all the more important to ensure that eldercare continues to be underpinned by respect for older people's rights and dignity. Producing something that has the potential to be helpful to as many people as possible, when work settings and learning needs will be different for all, has not been an easy task, but I have chosen to address that by focusing on 12 themes and sets of values that I feel are particularly significant in terms of underpinning best practice in eldercare. Forgive me for not covering everything, that was never my intention, and feel free to use the structure of this manual to explore any additional themes or issues that you feel inspired to after working through it. After

DOI: 10.4324/9781041054481-1

all, the main purpose of the manual is not to tell you what to do, but to encourage you to be a thinking practitioner.

I want this manual to serve as a reminder that the older people who need our support are not different from, or of less worth than, any other members of society, even though the ageist messages we often hear try to convince us otherwise. In the interests of challenging negative assumptions about older people, each chapter will focus your mind on a particular values issue by highlighting something about older people which sometimes gets forgotten or sidelined – something which shouldn't be assumed to be irrelevant because of someone's age but, unfortunately, often is. Each begins with some background material about the topic to fill you in with the basics if this is new ground for you, and to provide further food for thought, even if it is something you have already read or thought about. There is also an exercise that will help you to explore your thoughts on how you do, or could, ensure that how you support the people you do reflects an understanding of them as adult citizens in need of some help to live the life they want to live, rather than as people who have lost that status purely on the grounds of advanced age or frailty. In each chapter you will also find a tip that I have picked up along the way and want to share, and also some feedback from older people themselves on how they have experienced life in old age, and eldercare support. These will be featured as 'From Where I'm Sitting' comments. They are all based on real-life scenarios or constructed to reflect commonly shared experiences that have been recounted to me by the people with whom I have worked over the years.

This is not a textbook as the focus is intended to be on practice, rather than on an exploration of theoretical ideas. But that is not to suggest that eldercare practice, and the eldercare knowledge base which informs it, are two different and unrelated things. As Neil (Thompson, 2017) comments:

> the approach adopted is one of starting with practice and therefore lived experience, and using theoretical insights to develop an understanding of it, rather than the traditional technical rationality approach of trying to take a theory and apply it to practice. What should be happening in critically reflective practice is that we look carefully at the situation and seek to illuminate it by drawing on relevant parts of the professional knowledge base and integrating these into a meaningful whole that is applicable to the current practice situation.

(p. 25)

That is, when we are faced with a practice dilemma, or whatever, we stop and think about what we know that could help us to understand what is going on, what might be preventing progress and what a helpful way forward might be. If you find references to theory confusing, then try replacing the word 'theory' with 'knowledge'. It certainly worked for me at a time when I struggled to understand the concept and was tempted to not think about it and its significance!

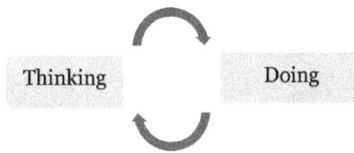

Figure 0.1 What informs your practice?

You might be asking yourself why, if your job is about *doing* eldercare, there is any need to worry about thinking unless you are enrolled on a course or aiming to get some sort of qualification. But, taking a step back from the 'doing' element of practice, if we consider that, if the 'rules' of how you do your job are just plucked out of thin air, or are based on your own or someone else's personal whim, then they run the risk of not being open to challenge and, as a consequence, can become resistant to change. For example, it is not uncommon for a culture of 'we'll do it this way because that's what we've always done, or what we've been told to do', to develop and persist, even if those rules, regimes or practices have been challenged at a number of levels as being inefficient, harmful, degrading or disempowering. So, for that reason, in each chapter, you will get the opportunity to read around the topic a bit before doing some thinking of your own   that is, to think about the implications of what you have read for your own practice. The content of this background material will vary, as what informs how we best support those with whom we work comes from a variety of sources, including academic writings, research, practice guidance, our own experience, feedback from those on the receiving end of our support, and so on. The extent to which you are already engaging with the ideas that inform the work that you are doing will vary too, but I hope that the material covered, if not new, will still provide food for thought and a basis for thinking about how it relates to you and your own circumstances. You might already consider yourself to be on a learning journey, having been given the opportunity, or created it for yourself, to explore ideas about practice, and your own thoughts on those ideas. Or it might be the case that you are being expected to provide support to older people without much in the way of guidance in terms of key principles of good practice – as if these are 'common sense' and don't need much thinking about. Perhaps you have had little opportunity to explore your own feelings about the work you are doing, and how you might make sure that your practice is the best it can be in the interests of both the people you support, and your own self-esteem and pride in your work. But regardless of where you are on your learning journey, be it at the very beginning or some way along it, the structure of this manual should work for you because it is designed to be adaptable to *your* circumstances and to stimulate *your* thinking about *your* practice. That is not to say that you have to do all the thinking on your own, as having discussions with others can be mutually helpful, but don't lose sight of the fact that it is indeed *your* journey and, while others can contribute to your learning, no one can do it for you.

As previously mentioned, this manual is not intended to be a set of instructions, as to think of eldercare in that way would be to deny the complexity of human life and to support the assumption that all older people are the same and can be 'processed' (as if they are 'things' or 'tasks to be done'), rather than supported to live the lives of their own choosing. What it *is* intended to be is an opportunity for you to think about what is guiding your practice – that is, not just to do, but to think about how and why you do what you do (or don't do for that matter). Incorporating ongoing learning and reflection into your practice is something that underpins professional practice. In some jobs it can be enough to learn basic procedures and sets of rules and to never revisit them because they equip you to do the tasks that are required of you as long as you remain in that job. But when you are working with people, and in particular with people who need a lot of help, then such an approach is not appropriate because, if you don't take on board developments in the field of people work in general and social care in particular, and think about how you can do your job as well as you possibly can in what are often difficult circumstances, then both you and the people you support are likely to lose out. A professional approach based on a commitment to ongoing development will help guard against this but, for this to happen, you need to consider yourself to be a professional and, in my experience, some people working in care situations don't see themselves as professional workers. They consider people such as teachers, lawyers, social workers, counsellors and so on as professionals, but not themselves. However, as your practice as a social care worker draws on knowledge, skills and values (a hallmark of professionalism) then you can lay claim to being a social care professional and should strive to keep that status.

There will be an expectation that you engage with the exercises, hear the perspectives of older people as their voices are expressed in the 'From Where I'm Sitting' stories, and at least be open to considering the usefulness of the tips shared. It is, of course, up to you whether you do so, but I hope you will. It will involve effort on your part, as it is your own response to what you read or experience that counts if you are committed to having what you learn feed into your practice, but effort that I hope you will find worth it. I certainly hope that, if I am ever in need of support, I am helped by someone who has made the effort to reflect on what can help them become the best practitioner they can be.

And maybe you would too?

Why a manual?

As I have already mentioned, my aim is not to provide you with all the information you need to be able to do your job well – that would be too big an undertaking. Instead, it is to provide you with an opportunity to *process* what you will read in the following pages, and what you will be picking up from other sources – that is, to give some thought to whether, and how, what you come across has relevance for the work you do, and how you do it.

Taking in information from reading, watching presentations, attending training courses, observing how colleagues work, and so on is all well and good, but its impact is likely to be short lived if that information isn't processed by considering the *implications* of that information for your own circumstances and intentions. For example, reading a policy which states that the care your employer provides will be dignified care is one thing, but what does that look like in practice? Without processing that information – thinking it through – how will you know whether you are upholding it or not? Do you and the person you are supporting agree on what constitutes dignified care, for example?

For each of the 12 chapters, the manual will guide you to consider the information provided (itself compiled largely from practice wisdom) by providing exercises and food for thought about its relevance for your own practice. I hope that you will not feel restricted by its scope and that you will consider it to have a life beyond the issues covered, in the sense that it will also provide a framework for helping to establish, or further develop, practice habits that incorporate thinking as well as doing. In turn, this will give you the confidence to draw out the implications for practice from sources of information you will come across in the future.

How do I use it?

The best answer I can give is to use it in the way that works best for you, as we all learn in different ways, and are more receptive to processing that learning at different times of the day and in different environments. In order to work out what might suit your style, I suggest that you read it through from start to finish initially. This doesn't need to be an in-depth read, just a skim through to get a feeling of what is being covered and would not include doing the exercises, but it should serve to give you an overview of what the manual is about, and the nature of the project you will be embarking on when you are ready to start engaging with the material more fully. It isn't necessary to work on the chapters in the order I have presented them, and when you work on it, and how much time you spend on it, are also entirely up to you. It might be that, due to personal, family or work commitments, you could struggle to create time to devote to study or contemplation without being interrupted. If that is the case, you might find it handy to use your notebook (or perhaps your phone) to jot down a word, concept or whatever has attracted your attention, so that you can return to it later when you have more time or energy. Without such a trigger, your 'light bulb moment' or the question you want to ask may be forgotten about and a valuable learning opportunity lost. It is designed to be an aid for your own reflection, and a guide or companion for your own learning journey, so use it in a way that works for you. It is *your* thinking space. Share your thoughts with others if you want to, or keep your reflections private if that's what you prefer. The most important thing to take on board is that reflection is crucial so don't let unease about how to do it and record it stop you.

I suggest you use a notebook alongside the manual so that you can record your thoughts on the material and the questions posed in the text. I hope you will take me up on that because many people feel that writing things down helps them to order their thoughts and, as a bonus, you will then have a resource that you can return to in the future – and one that you can add to and amend as you continue on your own learning journey. The format is for you to decide. For example, you might use your notebook to record in some depth your thoughts about something you've witnessed or done, as part of a process of thinking things through. Or you might want to just jot down key points. Or, if you have been inspired by the tips, to add some of your own or remind yourself of useful tips provided by others. Or a combination of these and more. Whatever works for you to achieve what you are setting out to do.

I have only one request in relation to how you use it. If you are serious about developing into the best eldercare practitioner you can be, then don't skip the exercises and do make some notes that are personal to you and your circum-stances. I'd like to think that the discussion sections provide some useful and relevant general material on the topics being explored but, if you don't move beyond that 'taking information in' stage to the 'what are the implications for this in my own practice' stage, then you won't be getting the full benefit of this aid to learning. And that would be a shame for everyone, not least those people you support. So now to the first of those important, but often overlooked, things to remember about old age and people's experience of it.

The older people you support are unique, not just 'one of the elderly'

We are *all*, of course, unique individuals and that applies just as much to older people as it does to any other age group. That might seem like an obvious comment, but it is something that can easily be lost sight of, especially if we work with people who have similar health conditions, or combinations of health conditions, such as strokes, dementia, heart failure and so on. When most of our work time is spent with people who need our support because of frailty associated with such conditions, it can become all too easy to think of people *as* their condition, rather than as individuals who happen to *have* those conditions. Where that happens, we can be seduced into thinking of a unique individual as just another old person, especially if we don't get much time or opportunity to build up a relationship with that individual in order to get a sense of who they are, what their life has been like up to that point, and what their hopes and plans for the future are. Under pressure of work it can become all too easy to fall into the trap of letting our practice become standardised instead of personalised – that is, to sometimes slip into a 'one size fits all' approach where we forget that we are working with unique individuals, rather than a 'unit of the elderly population'.

What doesn't help in terms of appreciating uniqueness is that when we get to interact with a particular person for the often short time that we do, we only get to see that person at a particular point in their life. It is as if we only get to see that person as a snapshot – a moment in time – and not necessarily a moment which reflects their individuality and the diversity of their life experiences. What also doesn't help is that ageism, a set of ideas which promotes the stereotype of older people as all being the same, and all being somehow of less worth than other adults, is a very prevalent one in our society. Later, we'll look in more detail at ageism, and how we might guard against its influence, but first let's explore uniqueness itself a bit more.

DOI: 10.4324/9781041054481-2

Uniqueness

Though we are individuals, unless we choose to live as hermits, we live in societies and interact on a daily basis with other individuals. It would be difficult for societies to function without there being some 'reining in' of individuality – for example, there needs to be a shared agreement on what constitutes acceptable behaviour – but we remain individuals nevertheless. To an extent, we can consider ourselves to be like other people, in that we may share a gender, ethnic or class background, and have shared experiences (for example, having lived through eras characterised by war, economic boom or collapse, social instability, rapid technological change, and so on), but no other person will share the exact combination of factors that have contributed to our life experience. And that is where our uniqueness lies.

As we see below, ageism works in a number of ways, and at different levels, to 'paint out' the uniqueness of individual older people's lives. They may have been fathers, mothers, husbands, wives, prime ministers, suffragettes, shopkeepers, sex workers, explorers, convicts, media celebrities to name but a few, but, on being defined as 'an older person', it is often the case that it is only their age that is seen as significant from that point on. Look at this from your own perspective. Imagine having little or no attention paid to, for example, your gender, or to the customs and values you hold dear in your particular ethnic or religious communities, or to your interests, or to the values that have underpinned your life choices. How satisfied would you feel in being treated like this? That we are not all the same is reflected in the term 'diversity', and the significance of this for how sensitively and fairly we are able to support those older people that we do is something we'll return to soon. But, given how significant a force it can be in terms of the potential to overlook or deny uniqueness, let's now look in a bit more detail at ageism.

TIP! Try turning the spotlight on yourself from time to time. Imagine how you would feel if you overheard someone you support saying 'I don't care who comes to help me today. It'll be a carer, that's all'.

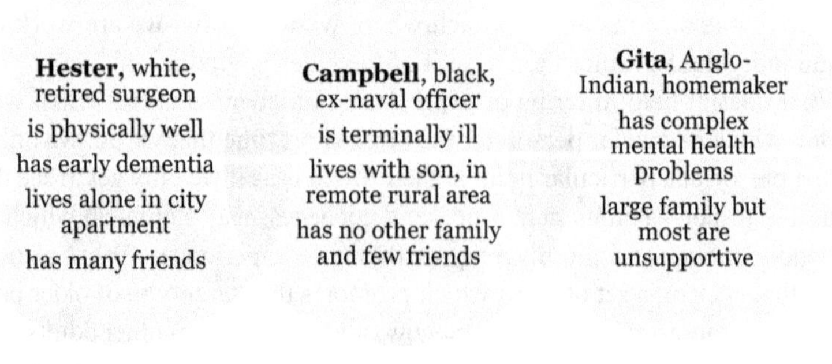

Hester, white, retired surgeon
is physically well
has early dementia
lives alone in city apartment
has many friends

Campbell, black, ex-naval officer
is terminally ill
lives with son, in remote rural area
has no other family and few friends

Gita, Anglo-Indian, homemaker
has complex mental health problems
large family but most are unsupportive

Figure 1.1 Uniqueness

Ageism

Ageism amounts to discriminating against people (treating them less favourably than others) on the grounds of their age alone. This applies to anybody, at any age, who finds that their age is being used against them, so it can apply to children and young people who find that their life experiences and opportunities are affected by unfair negative stereotyping. However, it is particularly applicable to older people, given the long-standing history in the UK and elsewhere of devaluing the role of older people in society, and of writing them off as 'past it'. An important point to recognise when it comes to ageism, is that age discrimination is a very common aspect of our day-to-day lives and the society we live in. We don't have to look very far to see examples of negative stereotypes of older people. Greetings cards for people over 60 often paint old age in a negative light, for example. And while racist and sexist comments are increasingly not being tolerated morally and legally, referring to older people as 'wrinklies' or 'old fogeys' and other such demeaning terms, doesn't appear to attract the same degree of disapproval. Consequently, if we are not careful to recognise, and guard against, making ageist assumptions and promoting ageist stereotypes, there is a very strong danger that we will reinforce them, even if we don't intend to.

We need to be on our guard because ageism incorporates a whole set of ideas (an 'ideology' or particular way of looking at the world and how we operate within it) that work 'behind the scenes' to portray this state of affairs not only as how things are, but as how things *should be*. And more than that, these ideas can be seen to reinforce each other to perpetuate the assumption that older people are almost like a different species from younger adults, rather than adults who are just further along their life's journey than younger people are.

I used to work with a doctor who was very aware of ageist assumptions and was very keen to challenge them whenever he encountered anyone who acted in a way that suggested that they were either not aware of age discrimination in healthcare or were choosing to condone it. If he came across a comment (or action) which he regarded as ageist, he would ask: 'Would you speak (or act) like that if this person were 30 years younger?' This proved to be a very effective way of identifying the ways in which we can be drawn into making negative and discriminatory assumptions about older people because of the ageist stereotypes that are so well-established and influential to our thinking.

From Where I'm Sitting: Stan's Story

I'm really pleased with myself. After a lifetime of enjoying learning about the world around me I finally got around to doing some formal studying. I'd always been too busy before, what with earning a living and then doing so much volunteering at the donkey sanctuary. In fact, it has only been since I got so short of breath and had to slow down that I gave some thought to doing some studying. It used to be more difficult for people in their 'later years' shall we say but now, with all these opportunities for distance learning, I've spent most of my 80s working towards getting the geography degree I've always hankered after. It has been hard work but a blast too, and I'm really looking forward to the degree ceremony. I'm hoping to have enough guest tickets to invite my carers. What I'm not enjoying, though, is all the attention I've been attracting – not for getting a degree, but for getting a degree at my age. The family are saying it, the local paper want to do a report on me getting a degree at 88 years old, and even the university people are making a fuss. They're making out I've done something extraordinary. Just goes to show what people expect of 88-year-olds if they think that this is something extraordinary. To be honest, for me it's taken the shine off my achievement because it feels more than a bit patronising, however well meaning everyone is.

Diversity

Diversity is about variety and difference. On the face of it, it seems a bit obvious to say that the world we live in is characterised by variety and difference – for example, differences relating to gender, class, disability, ethnic background, religion, sexuality, worldviews and so on. But what we need to consider is whether that diversity is seen as a problem for society, or something that enriches it. That is, we need to consider the value judgements that are made about difference (that is, the view that 'different' means 'less than'), and not just the fact that those differences exist. Neil Thompson (2021) highlights how the 'diversity approach' in social care supports the view that difference should not be seen as a rationale for discrimination:

> The fact that there are differences across ethnic groups, identities, approaches and perspectives should be seen as a good thing, a source of learning, variety, stimulation and interest, rather than a source of unfair discrimination based on 'punishing' some people for being different from the perceived mainstream.
>
> *(p. 14)*

Where older people are concerned, the potential for them to be discriminated against on the grounds of difference is magnified because, not only will diversity *within* the elderly population continue to attract unfair attention, there is also a tendency for them to be seen as different (and, by association, 'less than') in relation to people who are younger than them. So, for example, being a poor, black, disabled woman can be enough of a struggle because she is likely to face discrimination in relation to her gender, ethnicity and disability throughout her life, and this unfairness will not go away as she reaches old age. Instead, the potential exists for discrimination on the grounds of age to add yet another negative dimension to her life experience. And what has the potential to make things worse is the ways in which ageism works to distract attention from these matters by promoting the idea that once we reach old age, it is only our age that is seen to have any significance. As we will discuss later, in Chapter 6, older people have a wealth of experience and knowledge which has the potential to enrich the lives of others within and across generations and sectors of society, but we can see ageism working when this diversity, and the promise it offers, remains hidden behind the powerful, but inaccurate, stereotype of older people as frail, forgetful, and so on – the 'old fogeys' we see referred to so often.

In conclusion, I hope that working through this section has encouraged you to explore your role – and to keep on exploring it – and the potential it holds for you to be able to contribute very significantly to making sure that those older people who need help can have that help provided in a way that shows an appreciation of, and a respect for, their individuality and unique circumstances. That is, when we are supporting an older person, we place the emphasis on the *person* rather than the *older*. Perhaps now would be a good time to make some notes in your notebook? Maybe you have made a start already? I would suggest that you keep this manual in an easily accessible place after you have worked through it and, from time to time, revisit the notes you have made and reflect on how your understanding, and the application of that understanding to your practice, have developed over time. Remember that this manual is designed to support *your* learning journey, one that hopefully won't end when you've finished working through it.

Exercise 1

Take a sheet of paper (A4 or similar) and draw a vertical line down the middle to divide it into two columns. Head one column 'standardised practice' and the other 'personalised practice'. Under the title 'standardised practice', think of an example you have come across where an aspect of eldercare provision could be described as standardised, as in a 'one size fits all' approach. One example to get you thinking might be that of, in some nursing and residential homes, and long-stay wards in some hospitals, having a target of getting everyone into their beds by a particular time, perhaps before a shift change. Then, under the heading 'personalised', consider how that aspect could be managed in a way that respects uniqueness and choice.

Try and think of as many examples as you can of where you have observed standardised care provision and think about what would need to change for it to be considered an example of personalised care. You could, if you wish, do this exercise the other way round. If you can provide examples of personalised care practice that respect individuality, then consider what it is that contributes to that. What would the 'standardised' version look like?

Over to you ...

What steps can you take to help you always to remember that the older people you support are unique individuals, not just 'one of the elderly'?

CHAPTER 2

The older people you support are multi-dimensional adults

We have seen that it is not unusual for older people to be defined by their age alone, and to have their life choices underpinned by other people's expectations of how older people *should* live, what they *should* or *should not* aspire to, and so on. Because, as carers, we most often enter older people's lives in response to a need for help to live those lives, the first impression we tend to get of someone is of their physical dimension. That is, there is usually some sort of impairment – something not working properly, or some illness or weakness that means that the older person isn't able to do everything they need to do to live the life they want to be living. I'm sure we're all aware, if we think about it, that human beings have more than one dimension, that we are more than our physical bodies, but one of the consequences of ageism is that old age tends to be equated with physical decline, and only that. The term 'medicalisation' refers to the tendency for old age to be equated with sickness and the sick role, even though, in reality, it is only some older people who are sick or frail. You only have to think of the many people who have retained their health and vitality well into old age to put paid to that myth, but it still remains a powerful and persuasive one.

Dehumanisation

We are all human but we are more than our physical bodies. We are people, rather than things, and have more than one dimension. These, in combination, go towards making up our unique identities – that is, our 'personhood', what it is that makes me 'me' and you 'you'. If those aspects of our personhood are overlooked, then the effect is one of dehumanisation – that is, a process whereby a person, or group of people, becomes thought of as 'not human' or 'less than human'. And where this

DOI: 10.4324/9781041054481-3

is deemed acceptable in a society, it also becomes seen as acceptable to treat those people and groups with less respect, to deny or overlook their human rights, and so on. So, we have to rise to the task of doing what we can to challenge the myth that older people are just old bodies. If we begin to question terms such as 'the elderly' and 'the old', which are often used to describe a group of people as if they are all clones of each other, we can see that they say something about the difference *between* them and younger groups, but nothing about the differences *within* that grouping. For example, they do not give us an idea of the person's class, or gender, or ethnicity. They give nothing away about sexual orientation or religious allegiance or the language(s) they use. They tell us nothing about the person's life experiences, roles, identity or experience. And yet those terms are often the only ones by which people are referred to, as if nothing else but their age is significant.

So what other dimensions of humanity should we be considering if we are to treat those we support with the care they deserve as fellow human beings? Unfortunately, there isn't space here to explore every dimension so let's look at just two of them. Don't let that stop you exploring others – such as the psychological and emotional – under your own steam though, or in discussion with colleagues or managers, or both. While the physical dimension is a hugely significant one, especially in the sense that a lot of older people come to need support because of physical impairments or conditions, I would suggest that there is a wealth of material out there that will provide you with information, and food for thought, about your role. I am choosing, instead, to focus on two aspects that I consider to be hugely significant, but which are often overlooked or given less attention than they deserve in relation to older people and eldercare. These are the sexual and spiritual dimensions of their lives.

The spiritual dimension

Although spirituality is often associated narrowly with religion, it isn't something that is only about the belief in, or worship of, a higher entity, or adherence to a particular lifestyle in accordance with a particular set of teachings. What I want us to consider here is spirituality in the broader sense which relates to whatever it is that gives meaning to a person's life. For some, religion can be what gives life meaning by providing a set of beliefs or an ethical framework to live by but, for others, it might be something else that makes their life meaningful – a respect for the environment, for example, or being central to one's family or community wellbeing. Our spiritual dimension incorporates our understanding of who we are, what we consider our place in the world to be and, given that we rely on feedback from other people to construct our own sense of identity, our sense of worth in the world we live in. It is about 'big' questions – the who am I? why am I here? what is my life all about? – type of questions we grapple with on our spiritual journey through life. When things are going well in our lives, such internal 'self-evaluation' often fades into the background, but at times when we face a challenge of some kind – something that unsettles us because it causes us to question what we had previously considered to be 'certainties' in our lives – such soul-searching or 'internal conversations with ourselves' come to the fore. At such times, our spiritual need to feel 'grounded' can become very significant to us, and we look to others for support and comfort. If we don't get that support, or the recognition that such a need exists and is important to us, then this can add a further dimension to our 'conversations with ourselves', such that we can begin to question what other people think about our worth.

> **TIP!** When you first start your working relationship with an older person make it your business to find out, as soon as possible, what it is that makes his or her life meaningful.

If we think about the times in our life when we typically face spiritual challenges – those that cause us to question who we are, and so on – then we could include moving from childhood to adolescence, young adulthood to middle age, or middle age to old age. These transitions are not just about reaching a particular age or stage, but also, and more importantly in terms of our spiritual dimension, about what those transitions *mean* to the individual experiencing them. And because we live our lives as individuals, but within a social context where there are 'rules' and expectations about how we should relate to each other, the sense we make of those transitions is very likely to be influenced by other people's attitudes and expectations of what is 'appropriate' in terms of behaviour and aspirations for any particular phase of life. Societies can be described as ageist when policies and practices promote, or fail to challenge, the assumption that it is acceptable to treat people differently, and less favourably, purely on the grounds of their age and without any reference to competence or entitlement. It should not be hard to work out, then, that an older person living in an ageist society is likely to face quite a challenge to their self-image and self-worth. Imagine feeling that you matter, but having it reflected back to you that you don't. And yet that is what many older people experience, even though they may be making very valuable contributions at a number of levels, some of which we'll explore in more detail in Chapter 6 where we'll focus on reciprocity or 'giving back'.

This is a topic that deserves much more attention than we are able to focus on here but I hope that this very basic introduction has at least convinced you that the spiritual dimension of the lives of the older people you support is a key one because it is at the heart of what it is that makes them the person they consider themselves to be. I hope you will have been inspired to play your part in addressing the relative lack of attention given to the significance of spirituality (in its broader sense) in eldercare by helping the older people you support to live lives that are spiritually enriched, rather than spiritually diminished. That is, where they can continue to learn, grow, participate and make a positive difference rather than experience life as the world closing in on them, and their place in it become increasingly insignificant – the difference, perhaps, between living life and waiting to die?

The sexual dimension

This is another important dimension of all our lives and, as such, it should feature in discussions about good quality eldercare but, unfortunately, tends not to. The sexual dimension of our lives incorporates a number of issues, so let's begin by clarifying what we mean by it. It can be understood in terms of a person's sexual orientation, but also the reality of people's sex lives, experiences and relationships. As the older people we support are still people, despite what ageism would have us believe, I hope you'll agree that the following issues are as relevant to them as to anyone else:

Sensuality and physical intimacy Sensuality literally means the enjoyment of pleasure gained through one's senses. It is often associated with the intimacy involved in gratification of sexual needs, but it can refer to the pleasure to be gained from just feeling desirable, and from physical touch in itself. Realising that opportunities for physical closeness may be becoming less accessible as we become older can be a hard pill to swallow, given the effect it can have on one's confidence and sense of self-worth. It is therefore very sad that physical intimacy between older couples is more often the butt of jokes than a serious issue deserving of respect and sensitivity.

Emotional intimacy Closeness in relationships is not necessarily just about satisfying 'bodily' pleasures. At times when we are frightened, ill or worried, having an intimate closeness with someone can be a great comfort. If we think about sexuality just in terms of sexual needs and sexual encounters, then we can overlook the part that our emotions play within relationships. Sexual and emotional needs are interconnected, but physical closeness can satisfy both, independently of each other. A hug, or being cuddled up in bed together, can have a very beneficial effect on one's mood – it can be enough just to know that someone close to you knows what is worrying you and cares enough to show it.

Romance and relationships A sense of romance, although perhaps sounding sentimental to some people, may be an important part of a person's life. Even where someone is not physically capable of a full sexual relationship, the value and appeal of a romantic relationship with someone can be quite significant. We should therefore be careful not to underestimate the part that romantic feelings and relationships can play in people's lives – and that includes older people just as much as anyone else.

Sexual orientation Though there are signs, in some societies at least, that a variety of sexual orientations are being considered as at least morally, if not legally, 'acceptable', it is still the case that many people (particularly those who have grown up in less enlightened times) will have experienced, and maybe remain fearful of experiencing, social disapproval, ridicule or other forms of discrimination. Creating a safe and non-judgemental space to discuss aspects of their sexuality is something we should strive for if we are not to dehumanise older people because their sexuality is part of who they are and what they do as human beings.

From Where I'm Sitting: Ian's Story

I've been at Brightways ever since I had my spinal injury and it looks like I'll never make it back home now. Wasn't a wise move to buy a house in such an isolated place but there we are – you don't see such things as this coming, really. My partner, Mared, is younger than me – I'm 80 and she's 68 but in many ways she struggles more than I do – panic attacks and such. We'd been a good team up until this happened. She helped me do stuff when my pain was bad and I'd help her through the times when things just got too much for her. I worry about her living on her own now, though it helps having a phone in my room so she can ring day or night if she needs any reassurance or just wants some 'pillow talk' even though our actual pillows are in different places. I'd love to have Mared stop over here some nights – they're the worst time for both of us – but I don't think the staff here would understand. Perhaps they'd think that people our age are past all that? But we'd only have a cuddle, not that it should be any of their business anyway!

The point has been made that sexuality is an issue for all people, whatever stage of the life cycle they are at. It is an 'overarching' issue that cuts across age barriers, and so it is not one we can afford to ignore when dealing with issues relating to working with older people. However, it is important to note that there are issues about sexuality that relate *specifically* to older individuals and refer, for the most part, to the way in which they are perceived and stereotyped, and the problems which result from such distortions. These include:

Continuing sexuality Many adults will be part of existing intimate relationships when they become defined as 'old'. When these relationships last it is usually because the people involved want them to. So, why should advancing age be an issue?

Sexuality renewed Many people will not currently be in a relationship of intimacy, but we should be careful not to assume that this means that the door to such relationships is permanently closed. People can meet a new partner at any time of life, and so we should not allow ageist assumptions to lead us into taking it for granted that there will be no new relationships in older people's lives.

Sexuality lost Where sexual desire or vigour is lost there may well be a grief reaction. If it is not recognised as such, then the validation and understanding that many could feel supported by is unlikely to be forthcoming.

There are, of course, many more dimensions to human lives than we've had space to think about here, and any efforts you can make to develop a fuller understanding of what makes us multi-dimensional beings will help to ensure that, as a human being supporting other human beings, you appreciate what it is to be human and allow that understanding to inform the work you do. At the very least, I hope that working through this chapter will remind you that the older people you support remain the multi-dimensional adults they have always been, rather than become the one-dimensional stereotype of 'bodies in decline' that they are so often portrayed as. Grounding our practice in anti-ageist principles should help to ensure that we never get seduced by that influential, but inaccurate, portrayal of older people.

Exercise 2

Choose one of the people you support, or have supported, as the focus of this exercise. Under each of the following headings make brief, confidential, notes about how much you know about that dimension of his or her life.

Are there any dimensions that you know very little about? Consider whether it would be in their interests for you to understand these dimensions of their personhood more fully and, if so, how might you develop a better awareness? Are you entitled to this information?

Physical
Spiritual
Emotional
Sexual

Over to you ...
What steps can you take to help you always to remember that the older people you support are multi-dimensional adults?

The older people you support are still on a journey through life and not at the end of it

It is very likely that the people you support in your work will be quite a lot older than you are, but that just means that they are further along their life's journey than you are. And while you may assume that their journey will end before yours does, that isn't something we can take for granted. Much as we don't like to think about it, our own lives could end very suddenly and very soon and even before that of an older person with whom we are working. That said, do we spend much time thinking about how long we have lived and how long we have left to live? Unless we have had some sort of health scare, or have a crystal ball, the answer is probably no for most of us. The likelihood is that we just think of ourselves going about our business, getting older by the day, but not dwelling on it too much. But if we think about it, isn't that what older people are doing too – just carrying on along their life journey until such time as their journey ends at the point of their death.

And yet it is not uncommon for people (including the older person him– or herself) to think that, once they have become significantly dependent on other people, their 'useful' life has ended and that they have reached the end of their journey – just sitting in 'God's waiting room' as is often said – rather than still being on that journey. Without that crystal ball, or unless someone is planning to take their own life, we don't know how long the rest of our lives will be. Consider that, when we use the term 'for the rest of my life', we don't usually know how long that will be – it could be 30 years, 30 minutes or even 30 seconds. But however long or short the timescale of the rest our lives is, the same applies to everyone, regardless of their age, that we are always on a journey through life and have life lived but also life yet to live.

DOI: 10.4324/9781041054481-4

This has implications for how we can support the people that we do to live, as far as is possible, the life of their choosing. To use a travel analogy, to be the person who helps them on and off the trains that are going in the direction of where they want to reach, rather than the person who gives them a cup of tea in the waiting room while they wait for their hearse to arrive. I hope you agree that this topic is worth taking seriously, so let's explore it a bit more.

We are temporal beings

While it is generally the case that we are living in the moment, as it were, we should not forget that human life has a temporal dimension. That is, time is significant to us because we are always situated somewhere along a time continuum, with time behind us and time ahead of us. If we see a photograph of ourselves, we can appreciate that it records just a moment in time. Looking back at a collection of photographs of us at different points in our lives helps us to piece those moments in time together to make a narrative – or story – of our lives and to appreciate not only how we have changed, but also how other things have changed – cars, fashions, and so on. It can be fun, and also maybe sobering, looking at old photographs and thinking about what is different and what has remained the same since they were taken. It reminds us that life is not static and that we don't experience life as unchanging. We change, our surroundings change, social attitudes change, government policies change. The list of potential changes could fill the rest of this manual so we'd better stop there.

Consider, therefore, the extent to which photographs (which by their very definition just capture a moment in time) have limited use if we are aiming to understand a life lived. Imagine, for example, how you might feel if someone saw a photograph of you as a child chasing some birds round a park and causing them distress and then make the assumption that you have no respect for animal rights, even as an adult. 'Hang on a minute', you might say, 'that's unfair, I've changed a lot since then. That was just me at a point in my past'. And yet, it is not uncommon for older people to be seen as only and always old. I can remember being surprised as a young teenager to hear that the scar on my grandma's knee was not the result of an operation to replace an arthritic knee joint but the consequence, at age 16, of having got caught on a nail as she climbed over a fence trying desperately to get back into the house before the nine o'clock curfew imposed by her strict mother. Not only did she get a tongue-lashing (and maybe worse) for being out late, but also for ripping her dress and causing the expense of having a doctor be called out. I realised that I had only ever thought of my grandma as an old lady who made toffee for us and played the organ at the chapel. I'd like to think I could be forgiven for this oversight because of my young age at the time. I can now see though, that to forget that an older person has not always been at the point they are on the time continuum now, and will not remain at that point, is to apply different rules to them than we do to ourselves, which I hope you would agree is very unfair.

TIP! The people you support might well share some of their life history with you and this should help you to better understand their present life and how they cope with it. Use this as a trigger to ask them about life left to live and whether there is anything you can do now to help them reach a goal they haven't yet achieved but would like to.

Living while we are dying

Though many of us don't like to think about it in those terms, none of us is immortal and we're all going to die at some point. This means that we're all dying while we're living. Though it wouldn't do to be constantly having that at the forefront of our minds, the very fact that we know we are going to die sometime can help us to get the best out of life while we still have it. That is, being death aware can make us more life aware in a sense. Irvin Yalom, a psychotherapist who worked with many patients experiencing death anxiety, offers the following advice:

> Keep in mind the advantage of remaining aware of death, of hugging its shadow to you. Such awareness can integrate the darkness with your spark of life and enhance your life while you still have it. *The way to value life, the way to feel compassion for others, the way to love anything with greatest depth is to be aware that these experiences are destined to be lost.*
>
> (p. 147)

You might have come across the premise, attributed to Dame Cicely Saunders who founded the Hospice Movement in the UK, that terminally ill patients, though they are nearing the end of their lives, are nevertheless still living those lives. That is, they are living while they are dying. To forget that is to deny them their humanity, to deny them the opportunity to still be the person they consider themselves to be or still want to become, however short a time their consciousness of life, the world, and their place in it lasts. Facing death more imminently than might otherwise be the case doesn't necessarily take the joy of living away. Indeed, for some, it might even sharpen the senses to the point where the joy of living becomes enhanced.

If we apply this philosophy of 'living while we're dying' to the situation of the frailer older people who rely on us for help to live life as they want to live it, we can perhaps better appreciate how being considered to be at the end of the journey – waiting to get off the train, as it were, rather than still being on it and enjoying the scenery – can feel. It is not uncommon for people to think of frail older people as 'the almost dead', but consider how it might feel from an older person's point of view to be thought of as dying rather than living – a pretty hefty blow to one's sense of self and self-worth I'd suggest. You might want to take time out here to think about the part you can, or do, play in helping those you support to *live*, rather than just survive.

From Where I'm Sitting: Siobhan's Story

I didn't go to school because my folks needed me to help on the farm but I so yearned to be able to go. It wasn't to be and I did what was expected of me and got married and helped manage a neighbouring farm. We had three boys who grew up into strapping young men, two boys who died when their cart overturned, and a boy and two girls who died of measles during that horrible epidemic. I lost my husband when I was 70 but stayed on in the farmhouse where there was still plenty I could do, though I was getting breathless with all these grandbabies to chase after. Everyone says I'm getting too frail for all this and the lads have just finished renovating one of the outbuildings to make a little bungalow for me and have helped me move in.

So now I've got some lovely carers coming in to help me get up and ready for the day and to get a shower. I need to be up early to keep in touch with all the goings on with the farm – I'm still a partner in the business after all. In the afternoons I do a lot of reading, especially about how people live in other parts of the world. That's always been an interest of mine and I especially worry about how kiddies are still being allowed to die when there are cheap and easy ways to save them. I know what it's like to lose little ones for lack of medicines and it breaks my heart that it's still happening in some parts of the world. The carers keep telling me to have a rest but while I've got life left to breathe I'll keep on campaigning for child poverty to be sorted if at all possible. I don't want to leave this world without having made a difference but I'll have to slow down a bit as I get so easily tired. Still, I can keep on badgering politicians with letters and emails I suppose. I can't imagine ever taking a back seat and being quiet – that's never been my style. I can't do much but I can make a noise alright!

Past, present, future

We've already talked about life having a time or temporal dimension – that is, we live life as a time continuum so that, for every point we are experiencing life in the present along that continuum, there will be time behind us (life already lived) and time ahead of us (life still to be lived). Let's think some more about the relationship between those different dimensions, and the implication this has for supporting older people.

You might be aware of, and indeed have been actively involved in, reminiscence work – that is, in helping people to remember and celebrate their past experiences. In doing so, those who support older people in the present can get a better understanding of their personalities and needs because they can appreciate how experiences in the past have contributed to how they are experiencing life in the present, and to the choices they make. For example, knowing that a

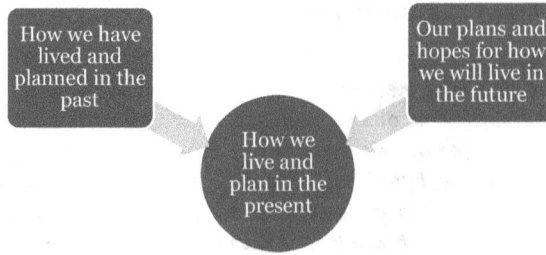

Figure 3.1 The significance of a future dimension

person had lived through wartime austerity in the past can go some way towards understanding their dislike, in the present, of food wastage. Or knowing that someone had spent a miserable childhood being 'the whipping boy' for a vicious and violent father, might help us understand why the welfare of that person's grandchildren in the present is of such significance to him, and why he has a tendency to put their needs before his own. The concept of 'cohort effect' is a useful one for helping us to appreciate that we have a shared experience (though not necessarily understanding) of historical events and public 'moods' with other people who are in the same age group (or cohort, to use the technical term). For example, I am in my 60s now and so probably share with others of *my* age cohort a tendency towards uneasiness about nuclear weapons because of having lived through an era where nuclear war seemed to be a real threat for quite some time. Take some time here to think about your own age cohort and how you, and others of a similar age, are experiencing life now, and how this might affect your expectations and fears when you all reach old age.

There is no doubt that the past feeds into the present and how we live our lives in the moment, and that this has been recognised for quite some time now by those in the field of eldercare who practice reminiscence or narrative therapies or life story work by encouraging dependent older people to revisit their past by, for example, looking at photographs, visiting 'old haunts' and so on, and sharing memories with others in their age cohort (Butler, 1963; Robinson and Hawranik, 2000; Kaiser and Eley, 2016). Such approaches are based on the premise that increased self-esteem can be promoted by helping older people to put the course of their lives in context, reminding them of what they have achieved over their lifetimes and how this has contributed to them being the unique and valued people that they currently are, even if they don't always recognise themselves as such.

This is to be welcomed, of course, but I would ask you to consider whether the relationship between the present and the *future* has been given sufficient attention. Do our hopes for the future not feed into what we do in the present too? Thinking about how what you want your future to be like affects what you do in the here and now. For example, wanting to have a financially secure old age in the future might influence you to pay into a private pension scheme now. Or an aspiration to get a nursing qualification – that is, something you aspire to be in the future – will affect choices you make in the present (working towards the necessary entrance qualifications, for example). But is it the case that frail older people, perhaps because they are often thought of as not having a future dimension to their lives (that is, they are deemed to be at the end of their journey rather than being still on it) are often not asked about aspirations for the future? And, if this is the case, does that not have implications for the supportive work we can do in the present? For example, if an older person aspires to still being able to play as active a role as they can manage in their neighbourhood for as long as they possibly can, what part can we play in supporting them to live their lives in the present to that end? I'll leave you with that food for thought.

Exercise 3

For each of the people you currently support, ask yourself the following questions:

Do I know what his or her plans for life left to live are? If not, how might I find out? Do I feel entitled to find out?

Are aspirations for the future spelled out on any documentation that I am given access to about the person's background, needs, preferences and so on? If they tend not to be included, why might this be the case?

What can I do to help make it more likely that this information would be sought and made available to me?

Over to you ...

What steps can you take to help you always to remember that the older people you support are still on a journey through life and not at the end of it?

CHAPTER 4

But some of the older people you support *might* be reaching the end of their journey

In this chapter we'll be looking at issues relating to supporting those older people who are close to the end of their journey through life and also their loved ones who are going through these final stages with them. Hospice care relates to the support given to people in the final months of their lives as an extension of the palliative care they may have received for many months, or even years, after receiving a prognosis that their condition has become incurable. Hospice is a service rather than a place and so, if you are working in this field, you may be working in a dedicated facility or, more likely given the finite number of hospice places available, in an older person's own home or that of one of their relatives, or in a residential or nursing home. In terms of the elements of values-informed care that we have explored this far – dignity, respect, choice, and so on – these will be as relevant here as at any other stage of life, and it is important too, perhaps more than ever, to remember and enact the principles of person-centred care in these circumstances. However, over and above these general principles, there are some issues that are particularly pertinent to end-of-life care and we'll explore some of these in the discussions that follow. As with all aspects of eldercare, there are many, many issues that we could consider but, because of lack of space here, we'll focus on just the following key issues:

- The older person's wishes;
- Keeping abreast of developments in the knowledge base;
- What constitutes a 'good death' and whether everyone has that option;
- Facing your own mortality;
- Confidentiality.

And so to the first of these: starting where the person is at.

DOI: 10.4324/9781041054481-5

The dying older person's wishes

If you, as a carer, are in the position of supporting a dying person, it is more likely than not that all those involved will have known that the death is imminent, or at least not far away. This will have given the dying person time to think about how they want to die (a 'death plan', you could say, in the same way as soon-to-be parents construct a birth plan). This plan might be a formal, written one, or perhaps one just outlined verbally to the significant people in the person's family or social network. Whatever form it takes, it will function as a means to let people know how they want to die, when they know (and maybe fear) that arrangements are likely to be beyond their ultimate control because of, for example, physical weakness, decline of mental acuity, the side effects of medication, and so on. They might specify, for example, that they want to die in a particular room in their house, or even in their garden or some other place that is special to them. They might want their whole extended family to be present for their final few days or hours, or just have one special relative, friend, or pet to be with them as they leave this earth, or even to be on their own. They might have compiled a playlist, as did a friend of mine, of 'music to die to', or just want to have the soothing sounds of nature – birdsong perhaps, or waves lapping on the shoreline, for example - playing in the background. Or, if they have been 'party animals' throughout their lives, they might want to die to the sounds of their favourite dance music played with the volume on high and the sound of glasses clinking and people obviously having fun. In an ideal world these wishes would always be facilitated but sometimes, if they don't chime with another family member's idea of 'how dying should happen' they might be downplayed or overlooked. Have you even been in the situation of being 'piggy-in-the-middle', as it were, in that you have been aware from your interactions with the older person who is dying that they want things to go a particular way, but someone else has other ideas? This can be a difficult position to be in, especially when family dynamics are strained and emotions are running high, but a commitment to person-centred practice can help you to keep your focus on, and being an advocate for, the dying person's wishes. It won't be your job to ensure that things pan out as the person you are supporting wants them to, but you will be in a good position to facilitate the crucial (and often missing) communication channels that need to be operating in such situations if the dying person's wishes are to remain paramount.

However, while we can look at things from a micro-analytical perspective, with its focus on interpersonal interaction, there is more to consider than individual preference and opportunity in terms of fulfilling a dying older person's wishes. If we look at the bigger picture (a macro-level analysis) we are alerted to the fact that not everyone has access to the resources that they hope would be in place to make their wishes possible. Poverty is a key factor here (Benatar, 2016). So, for example, while some older people and their families are helped financially and emotionally by charitable organisations and some government-sponsored health initiatives, access to this help is not guaranteed. Without the financial means to pay for the extra heating, bedding and so on that are often necessary when a person is dying, and to compensate for wages lost if a family member has to, or wants to, take time off work, issues relating to poverty can make an already difficult time even more difficult to manage. We can also see that differential access to support can be an issue in relation to different cultural requirements or preferences. If there is a mismatch between what members of a particular religious or ethnic group want in the way of support, and what is made available to them, then those people are unlikely to have their wishes met unless they have the support of members of their community who understand where they are coming from (and, indeed, going to) or can afford to pay for such care.

Have you found yourself in the situation of wanting to 'start where the older person is at' but have found that there are obstacles in the way of doing that – obstacles that are beyond your control? If so, how did you feel about that? Do you have strategies in place to help you deal with that reality? It can be helpful for all concerned to refrain from making promises because you might not be able to keep them. And even when the breaking of a promise is not your fault it may be perceived as such, especially when emotions are running high, and some people may be looking for a scapegoat to blame when they are trying to make sense of what they perceive as 'the unfairness of it all'. We'll return later to the matter of self-care but, at this point where we're considering a dying person's wishes, it is important that you don't put yourself at risk of disappointing others and demoralising yourself in the process.

From Where I'm Sitting: Chevy's Story

He is, or sadly was, 71 and I'm the opposite, 17. I've been a support worker at the hospice for a few months now and love every minute of it, even though it can wreck my emotions at times. I spent a lot of time with Griff as he never seemed to get any visitors. He told me that he'd been homeless for most of his adult life and that alcoholism, sleeping rough, and not eating well or much had taken a toll on his health. He knew how bad things were and fully expected to die soon because he'd been told that his heart, kidneys and liver had had enough and were giving up on him. He told his doctors that 'he'd had a good innings' though, to be fair, they said that it wasn't about old age but about his lifestyle. Apparently he'd resisted coming into the hospice for the end of life care he needed because he didn't want to be separated from his beloved dog, Maisie. He'd got her as a rescue dog several years ago and they had given each other the love and companionship that they both needed. He agreed to come in once it was made clear that Maisie could come with him and sleep next to him as she had done wherever he had found a place to lay his head.

Griff told me that he wasn't afraid of dying as long as Maisie was there for him to stroke as he left this earth. I made a promise to him that I would make sure that she would be with him, then went off to spend my weekend off with my mum. When I came back to work, I found out that Griff had begun to bleed very heavily and had been taken to hospital for urgent investigations, and that he had died there less than 24 hours later. I was distraught because I'd promised that he'd die peacefully at the hospice, stroking Maisie. My supervising colleague assured me that he probably hadn't been aware that Maisie wasn't with him but I'm not so sure. She said that I shouldn't blame myself but that, once I'd got over the shock, I might want to think about making promises that I might not be able to keep.

Keeping up with the knowledge base

In Chapter 7, I highlight the importance of keeping abreast of developments in the theorising of loss and grief and consider some of these and how they can offer useful insights into a) how people experience loss and grief and b) how we as carers can work in informed, relevant and sometimes innovative ways to support them. I am not suggesting that it is necessary for you, as a carer, to be an expert in all matters relating to death and dying but what I am suggesting is that there is a large and growing literature base out there which can, and should, inform your work if you want to be the best practitioner that you can be. Take advantage of the willingness of other professionals (and, of course, those older people and their families who use their services) who show themselves willing to share their knowledge and experience of matters relating to palliative and end-of-life care.

Current debates include:

- The legal and moral issues relating to 'assisted dying' and euthanasia;
- How palliative and end-of-life care should be funded;
- Whether it is enough to leave the compassionate leave needs of family carers of dying older people to the discretion of individual employers or should moral guidelines be incorporated into legal obligations;
- Whether the inequity that exists in hospice provision be addressed locally or nationally, especially in relation to the projected rise in the number of older people likely to die in the next few decades and whether ageism may influence whether they will be seen as having the same entitlement to a designated end-of-life pathway to support their dying as anyone else would.

These are just a few of the many debates and concerns that could have been highlighted and it may be that you have come across several others as you go about your business or watch the news. Nobody will be expecting you to be heavily involved in such debates, or even to declare an opinion. In fact, your employment contract may explicitly ban you from getting involved in public debates about government or departmental policies, for example. However, if your practice is informed by values and ethics, it is likely that problems and debates such as these will be of interest to you, and matter to you because they are about challenging what might get in the way of helping the people you support to have the best possible last few months, weeks and days of their lives. Though making the big changes that are necessary for end-of-life care to be made available universally and equitably will be beyond you as an individual, take some time here to consider how you might be able to contribute to informing the debates you come across. At the very least, your awareness of current issues and debates may help your working relationship with the person you are supporting, and their loved ones, who are probably aware of those issues themselves and may welcome your commitment to change, even if you can't make the changes yourself.

What is 'a good death'?

In terms of the commitment to person-centred care that underpins this manual, perhaps a 'good' death could be defined as one where the dying person's expressed wishes have been met? However, keeping the dying person's wishes, and their conceptualisation of a 'good death' at the centre of things is not always as easy as it sounds because the potential exists for there to be as many different perspectives on what makes for a 'good death' as there are people involved in the team supporting that person and his or her loved ones.

The fear that their own definition of a 'good death' may get lost in the mix, especially as they become more and more powerless to influence what is happening around them as they die, drives some people to make that personal definition of a good death known to others by formalising it into a document such as a living will. And while it might not always be possible to follow their directives to the letter, at least their wishes are made explicit and can inform the best possible practice in a given situation. That their wishes may not be followed when they are in a powerless position may be particularly concerning to an older person, given that ageism is a powerful ideology in relation to whose perspective carries most weight. They might understandably fear that they may become the victim of paternalistic interpretations of what their death should be like or of 'compassionate ageism' (Swift and Chasteen, 2021) whereby supporting the good quality care to which older people are entitled might, albeit unintentionally, reinforce the stereotype of older people as vulnerable and 'voiceless'.

Take some time here to reflect on whether you have been in a practice situation where you have seen a mismatch between understandings of a 'good death'. How did you feel? Did you think you had any power (or right) to intervene and point those differences out? Conversely, have you been in a situation where you have been proud to have helped enact a 'good death'? Can you identify what part you played in that and what did it do for your self-esteem?

If you search the literature base relating to 'a good death' you will notice that there is no absolute agreement on a definitive list of what makes for it, but there are some principles which seem to be common to attempts by different organisations to do so, including those relating to hospice care, where such principles are very evident in their value base. These include:

- Being comfortable – particularly in terms of pain management;
- Having trust in care providers;
- Not being a burden;
- Knowing that loved ones will be supported;
- Being in control.

For many people, that last one – being in control – is the most significant and I'm sure that you can see how it informs the ongoing debates about euthanasia and assisted dying, as these avenues can offer at least a degree of control when all other options for self-management of one's life have been exhausted.

So, as you understand it, is there equal access to a 'good death' as a dying person defines it? Borgstrom and Visser (2025) make reference to the fact that, in the UK at least, only approximately 4% of deaths can occur in hospices:

> If hospice care is deemed to be a 'gold standard' for the care of the dying, it is essential to question who can access this 'gold standard' and what structural barriers there may be to access.

(p. 75)

One has to wonder, then, how many of those scarce places are offered to older people, and whether age is one of those structural barriers.

TIP! We live our lives as individuals in a social context, but we die as individuals in a social context too.

Facing your own mortality

Living with, or visiting to support, a person who is reaching the end of their life has the potential to cause us to come face to face with the reality that we will all die at some point. Some people cope better with this revelation than others do but it is never easy and often *very* difficult to accept. In some situations, once the initial soul-searching processes have been worked through, it is possible to put thoughts about death and dying (particularly our own) to the back of our minds, only to be thought about again if we face a bereavement or have a health scare. But if you are working day in and day out with people who are nearing the end of their lives, your own mortality is something you are faced with on a very regular basis. Familiarity with an experience doesn't necessarily make it easier to bear and so, without strategies in place to help us deal with our feelings, rather than bottle them up or file them under 'for dealing with later', our own wellbeing is likely to be put at risk.

The psychotherapist Irvin Yalom (Yalom, 2008), in writing about the concept of death anxiety, makes the following comment:

> It's not easy to live every moment wholly aware of death. It's like staring the sun in the face: you can stand only so much of it. Because we cannot live frozen in fear, we generate methods to soften death's terror.
>
> *(p. 5)*

Papadatou (2009), in explaining the concept of relationship-centred care, highlights the extent to which end-of-life professionals, including carers like yourself who play an important role in supporting people, are not immune from the consequences of emotional investment:

> Such an approach invites professionals to understand not only the other person, but also the selves they bring to their encounters ... Expertise in palliative and bereavement care, although important, is not enough. No matter how "expert" we become – or strive to appear – dying and bereaved people remind us that we are human and equal in the face of death. We all die – some sooner, others later. In this field of work, we are all affected by the transience of life, the irreversibility of death, the suffering that loss engenders, and an existential quest for meaning.
>
> *(p. 13)*

Facing your own mortality involves finding a balance between being aware that life is finite, and not having that realisation dominate your waking hours or keep you awake at night. That is, to keep it at the back of your mind but not let it always be at the front of it. If you regularly work with dying people, have you ever been given the opportunity to discuss how you feel about your own future, to develop strategies to 'soften death's terror', or to de-brief if you have been in a situation where someone else's experience of dying has given rise to concerns about your own? If so, did this recognition and support help you, and how? If not, how might you get issues around facing your own mortality on the agenda for discussion?

And finally ...

A reminder about confidentiality

In your work as a professional carer respect for the privacy of the people you support is something that will surely have underpinned every aspect of your work because to betray someone's confidence is to betray their trust in you, and to suggest to them that their feelings and wellbeing don't matter – an example of the process of dehumanisation that we explored in Chapter 2. It is likely that, at a time when someone becomes critically ill, or it is known that they are nearing the end of their lives, you will be approached by people in their wider community to give them a progress report. While this may, and often does, come from a place of genuine concern, being asked to comment on someone's health puts you in a difficult position because you can appreciate their concern but your ultimate loyalty needs to rest with the older person you are supporting.

One way of avoiding this challenging situation is to remember the main principle of person-centred practice, which is to 'start where the person is at'. That is, to ask them to tell you what *they* want you to say when people ask about them, and who can be privilege to this information. By doing that, you will have a 'script' ready in advance of being asked. For example, you could say that you personally aren't allowed to comment, but if you ask person x they may be able to help you. In that way, the dying person retains control of confidentiality and you are relieved of the potential for transgressing it.

In conclusion, underpinning the issues we have explored here is the need to keep the person we are supporting at the heart of decision-making, but we have explored what can sometimes make this value commitment difficult to maintain at the very time when it can matter most that a person feels in control of their life still, and when everyone's emotions (including our own) are heightened and often raw. Though your primary duty will be to the person who is receiving end-of-life support, they will be going through that experience in the same context as they have lived their lives. That is, as an individual but an individual in a social context – family, community and so on – and in each situation you will be part of that context. Because you are supporting people but are a person yourself, you might sometimes feel that you are supporting everyone else too, just because you are part of a professional support network and are often in their presence. I have heard a lot of people who work in this field saying that, though the work is challenging, it is also a privilege. You might agree, but you might want to consider whether, in the work that you do, you remember the duty you owe to yourself and your own wellbeing.

Exercise 4

1. Make a list of the ways in which you have (or if you haven't worked in this field, might) made a contribution to preserving a person's dignity and sense of self-worth when they are at the end of their lives. This could include directly in a practice situation, or indirectly through your influencing of practice or policy.
2. Has anyone ever validated your contribution? If so, who? If not, might you consider asking for that, or at least for the chance to discuss it at a team level?

Over to you ...

What steps can you take to help you always to remember that the older people you support might be reaching the end of their lives?

CHAPTER 5

The older people you support are people *with* problems, not problems themselves

Consider how often you hear elderly people being described as 'a burden' or a drain on resources. With a worrying frequency, for example, we read about 'the problem' of bed-blocking in hospitals – that is, the situation where people are considered to be well enough to be discharged from hospitals on health grounds, but whose need for support to help them live safe and fulfilling lives in their communities cannot be responded to with any sense of urgency by the cash-strapped local authorities who are charged with that duty. We hear about how over-stretched care workers have so many older people to support over the course of each day that they have to look to ways of cutting corners, often compromising dignity, rights and sometimes safety (including their own), in order to get through the visits allocated to them for each shift. And we hear about how 'the problem' is only going to get worse because people are tending to live longer, but with the impairments that often accompany the ageing process.

So, inevitably, more older people needing hip replacements, more older people needing doctors' visits, more older people needing supported housing, more older people needing, needing, needing.

With all this emphasis on need, it can become all too easy to fall into the trap of *equating* old age with need and dependency. That is, to assume that if you are old, then you are, by definition, needy and dependent and, significantly for how you are perceived and treated, that this dependency is your only defining feature. These assumptions draw heavily on notions of dependency, regardless of evidence to suggest that old age is more often a time of independence, or interdependence, personal coping and, more than that, continuing personal growth. There is no shortage of evidence to suggest that the negative stereotype of older people as always frail and needy is not a true representation of life in old age.

DOI: 10.4324/9781041054481-6

Instead, the evidence indicates that the majority of older people go about their lives independently or with minimal support from family and friends – which is what most of us do if you think about it. Yet the negative stereotype is the one which so often wins out, which says something about the power that ageism has to influence us, and highlights why we need to guard against this.

It is often enough to just hear or read in the media about older people being described as a burden to fall into the trap of equating old age with dependency on welfare resources and to be persuaded to 'buy into' the assumption that it is older people who *are* the problem, rather than victims of policies that *cause* problems for them. But what can make things worse is that those of us who work in the fields of health and social care may well get an even more biased view because the assumption that to be old is necessarily to be dependent can become reinforced when all of the older people we work with day in and day out actually *do* need support. In these circumstances it can sometimes become difficult to think about older people in any other way, and to think of old age only in negative terms. However, this is not to say that a tendency to see older people *as* problems rather than people *with* problems can be explained away by just the views and actions of individuals whose practice is not rooted in anti-ageist values. That would be a very simplistic, and therefore unsatisfactory, explanation for what is a much more complex situation. To get a better understanding of why older people are often thought of as a problem, and one which can help us to work towards a more helpful solution for the older people affected, we need to look at processes that can be seen to be operating at levels beyond that of individual workers interacting with individual older people. One of these is how issues are 'problematised' – that is, come to be defined as a problem.

From Where I'm Sitting: Fernando's Story

Paulo should be here soon. He calls every day on his way from work and I don't know how to feel about that because it's something to look forward to but he's got enough problems without me being another of them. I know if I've had a bad day and forgotten to do something or got it all wrong as usual that he'll sort things out. So yesterday I made him a cake – something to focus on and something to say thank you, but that didn't end up well either. Sometimes I end up losing my grip on things and that isn't a nice feeling, I can tell you. And the thing I fear most is being a problem for him.

He says I'm not and that, even if I were, I've done loads for him, but I feel so useless. He's busy and shouldn't be needing to sort my muddles out when he's got enough to do with his own affairs. When he looked at the cake I could see it in his eyes that he wasn't keen on trying it – he said 'thanks, I'll have some of that later'. He probably gave it to the birds if he had any sense. I've thought about getting someone else to give me a hand but

I wouldn't know what to say if they ask me what I need help with – just being me is all I could say and I don't suppose they've got an answer for that problem.

Problematising

How we, as a society, address problems will depend on what the problem is assumed to be, and there are many takes on that. In relation to how we might best support older people, it is worth looking at just a few of these different perspectives on where the problem lies.

'The problem' is too many frail old people

How we, as a society, respond to a problem will depend on what the problem is perceived to be and who it is deemed to be a problem for. For example, if policymakers see a rise in the elderly population as likely to be accompanied by a rise in the amount of money that will need to be spent on health and social care, then they are likely to see it as a problem if budgets are already tight. This might then influence how they set about tackling what they have identified as 'the problem'. They might, and some local government organisations already have, make the eligibility criteria for entitlement to care provision more stringent, which allows for some people to be excluded from their sphere of responsibility, and therefore for the cost to the government to be reduced. That's one way of looking at, and responding to, 'the problem'. As a consequence, older people could be said to doubly lose out – not only are their needs not met, but they are also 'scapegoated'. That is, they're blamed for living longer and contributing to other people losing out! However, let's look at 'the problem' from a different angle.

'The problem is' that we make old people frail

From this perspective it could be argued that a lack of investment in things like town planning, transport, housing, community safety and so on contributes to the situation where older people find it more difficult to live independent lives without relying significantly on other people for help in doing so. For example, independence can be difficult to maintain in the face of policies which keep a lot of older people in relative poverty; fail to provide safe and accessible transport, particularly in rural areas; encourage businesses to trade from out-of-town retail parks which are difficult to reach if you don't own a car or are no longer able to drive; and so on. From this perspective, it is the policymakers who are the problem, not the older people.

'The problem is' that older people are different from ourselves and so need treating differently

From this 'take on things' the blame is again deflected away from older people, in that the problem is seen to lie with attitudes and assumptions about old age. When we are children, we are not expected to engage in civic life. We can't vote in elections, for example, because we are not considered to be mature enough to make decisions about how resources should be allocated, and so on. On becoming adults, we get given citizenship rights on the basis that we are mature enough to appreciate that, in return for taking our citizenship duties seriously, we will be given citizenship rights in return. That is, if we live our lives in a law-abiding and community-minded way, we will be entitled to expect that we be treated fairly and with respect for our dignity, and that we are allowed a share of the resources our society has access to.

However, as far as older people are concerned, this relationship between rights and duties is called into question if an assumption is made that old age is seen as a legitimate reason to take people's citizenship away from them. This can't be done legally but it can be done at the level of ideas and assumptions. Eric Midwinter, writing in 1990, introduced a very useful concept in this respect, that of 'post-adulthood'.

He uses this to refer to the assumption that, once adults reach old age they are presumed to no longer be full citizens, with all that this entails, but as somehow 'less than' other adults, and the adults they used to be. The implication of this is that, when people talk about issues such as the dignity and respect that adults should expect as a citizenship right, older people may be excluded from that set of expectations. And where they come to be perceived as 'less than adults', it becomes easier for some people to treat them as 'less than human' (which can pave the way for abuse) or on the same basis that they were treated *before* becoming adults (for example, calling them by their first or pet names without asking their permission to do so, as is seen to be acceptable in childhood).

Having looked at just a few of the different perspectives on what is a problem and for whom, we can see that these issues matter because how a problem is perceived, and for whom, will have implications for who needs to address it and how. You might want to consider that, where older people (and old age itself) are seen as a problem that needs addressing, this attitude will have consequences for how support services are designed and funded at a policy level, and therefore for how you are expected and enabled (or otherwise!) to deliver them. Potentially, these could include:

Forgetting, or minimising, the people element of 'care of older people' in policy and provision. That is, working from a starting point and mindset that older

CHILDHOOD – assumed incompetent to 'sign up to' citizenship rights and duties

ADULTHOOD – assumed competent to 'sign up to' citizenship rights and duties

POST-ADULTHOOD – assumed, on reaching old age, to have become incompetent to 'sign up to' citizenship rights and duties

Figure 5.1 Post-adulthood

people with support needs *are* a problem, rather than people *with* a problem, can lead to situations where care provision becomes 'service led' – that is, driven, to a greater extent, by the needs of the organisation providing or funding care – *their* problems, such as staffing, the logistics of timetabling and so on – rather than 'person led' – that is, driven, to a greater extent, by the needs of the older person who needs help to address the problems they face in their day-to-day lives.

Reinforcing the focus on dependency that figures strongly in ageist stereotypes

Very few older people are totally dependent on others, and it is more often the case that an older person will be dependent in some ways, but less dependent (or totally independent for that matter) in others. And, if we think about it, isn't that the case for most of us at whatever age we are? Where an assumption that older people are a problem to be dealt with persists, this can contribute to a tendency to forget about people's positive attributes and skills – what they *can* do as opposed to what they *can't* do, or struggle to do without help.

Raising an expectation that we play a part in safeguarding scarce resources

It is true that governments don't have a bottomless pit of money, but where older people are seen only in terms of being a draw on the economy, the ways in which they can, and do, contribute to it too can be overlooked. For example, by helping to raise and educate children, they can be a resource as well as a draw on resources.

TIP! Whenever you hear the word 'problem' being used – in any context, not just at work – give some thought to who is defining what is a problem and why. It can provide very interesting food for thought about who stands to benefit from proposed solutions!

I hope you'll agree that it is fair to say that we're *all* people with problems. And that we're all dependent on others at one time or another, and for a variety of reasons. For example, we might need some extra help with childcare responsibilities if we are recuperating from an operation or bout of illness. Or we might need a temporary financial loan to tide us over if we have been faced with an unexpected extra expense. Or we might need to call on the help of others in our community if our living accommodation gets damaged by an emergency like fire or flooding. Yet we're not all described as a burden, or a problem. We're more likely to be described as people with problems. Unless, it seems, we have reached that age when we come to be designated as old. In Chapter 1 we looked at how ageism is about treating people differently, and less fairly, purely on the grounds of their age. With that in mind, I'd like to think that raising our awareness of how what happens at the level of ideas, and how they spread and become influential, is something worth doing because it does have an impact on how people are able to live their lives as they wish to, and also to the extent we are able to help them.

You might feel that changing attitudes and policies is something that is beyond you as an individual worker, but treating each older person you work with as a person, not a problem, will mean that you are part of the change that you want to see.

Exercise 5

Think of a time when you have been made to feel that you were a problem. Perhaps an incident when you were a child at school, or as an employee? Or maybe as a customer buying a product that proved to be faulty, or a service that wasn't delivered to your satisfaction. Now ask yourself the following questions:

Did you get given the chance to challenge the assumption that *you* were the problem?

If so, what strategies did you use to persuade them that the problem didn't lie with you?

Does thinking about the situation you are analysing help you to appreciate how older people might feel when they hear themselves being referred to as a problem?

Might the strategies you used be useful for them in their challenge to that assumption?

Over to you ...

What steps can you take to help you always to remember that the older people you support are people with problems, not problems themselves?

CHAPTER 6

The older people you support are capable of giving as well as receiving

As we've noted already, one of the unhelpful stereotypes of older people is that they are, by definition, vulnerable and dependent. That is, they are needy. If we look at that negative stereotype more closely we can see that it is an inaccurate one, but that doesn't stop a lot of people from believing it to be true. Of course, older people *do* draw on society's resources, but don't we all? The extent to which they need some help from others may indeed increase for some people as they get older, but this is a far cry from assuming that old age is *necessarily* a time that is only characterised by dependency – that is, as a time when older people take but don't give back.

If we think about the course of our lives, we can see that there will have been times when we have needed to receive help from others (following an injury, for example, or a mental health crisis) and times when we have been able to be the ones doing the helping – a constant interplay called *reciprocity* which is all part and parcel of being a citizen of the society we live in. So, at times, we have all been a draw on society's shared resources (for our education, healthcare and so on) but will also have been able to contribute to those shared resources (as taxpayers and family caregivers, for example). That's what citizenship is about – a duty to give back to society as well as draw from its shared resources.

We can say, then, is that our lives are characterised by reciprocity and yet, though it remains important regardless of the stage of life we are at, it is an aspect of eldercare that isn't always given the attention it deserves, to my mind. So, let's look in a bit more detail at reciprocity and see whether you agree that it should.

What do we mean by reciprocity?

Reciprocity is about giving back, as exchange for receiving something. In most societies, it seems, it is an expected feature of interactions between people – what

DOI: 10.4324/9781041054481-7

is often referred to as a 'social norm' or shared expectation. If you think about sayings such as 'do as you would be done by' or 'behave towards others as you'd expect them to behave towards you' you'll get a sense of what reciprocity is – a sort of unwritten rule about how we should behave towards, and what we might expect of, each other.

Expectations of reciprocity can operate at many different levels. For example, at the level of international politics reciprocal trade treaties are bargained for to ensure mutual benefit for each of the nations involved. In a sense, that is what reciprocity is all about – mutual benefit, give and take. But it can be seen to be operating at the level of personal interaction too, such that we don't get far in our daily lives without giving something of ourselves or getting something from others. Sometimes it is a formal arrangement as in 'I provide a service for you and you pay me'. Or it can be to do with social arrangements as in 'I'll stay at home and raise children if, in return, I'm recompensed financially in some way by the government in exchange for not being able to earn a living'. But it operates informally too, as in situations where someone does someone else a favour just because they can, and because they'd hope that the person they're doing the favour for would do the same for them if they needed help at some point. In that sense, reciprocity can be used to describe a general sense of 'usefulness' in life.

Clearly, processes of give and take are a big part of social life, and that includes how older people experience life too, so let's think about this a bit more.

Why is being able to give as well as receive important?

There are many ways in which reciprocity can be seen to promote positive outcomes, not just for older people but for society in general, but we'll focus on just three of these here. Hopefully, thinking about these issues will inspire you to think of others:

1. In Chapter 2 we discussed how we should not forget that older people are multi-dimensional adults, and that one of those dimensions relates to their spiritual needs. If we accept that it is important to their spiritual wellbeing that older people feel that they are still valued citizens – that they *matter* – then we can see that being able to reciprocate, to give something back, is likely to be very significant to someone who has become dependent on others. If, throughout their lives, they have had their positive self-esteem reinforced by being considered competent, generous, or whatever, then to have this basis for feeling 'useful' taken from them can be experienced as a very significant loss. So, being able to be 'useful' in some way is important because of the implications for spiritual wellbeing – the sense of being a 'good person'.

2. Focusing on reciprocity as 'giving back' can help to challenge the commonly-held assumption that old age is all about decline and loss. Focusing on reciprocity can serve as a reminder that old age doesn't have to be all about

negativity. It can, and often is, a time of personal growth and development and of increased participation in civic affairs and social life, rather than withdrawal from them. So, opportunities for being able to give as well as receive are important because, with the potential they hold for being able to highlight what older people *can* do, rather than what they *can't* do, they can help portray a more positive portrayal of ageing than one which only highlights the negatives.

3.   It is important because it can reinforce the principle that a major feature of your role in supporting a frail older person is to empower them, to assist them to live, as far as is possible, the life of their own choosing – that is, to encourage a working relationship of give and take. So, they do what they can and you fill in the gaps. This can challenge the assumption that older people are presumed to be *either* needy (the take aspect of reciprocity) *or* competent (the give aspect of reciprocity), rather than a combination of both. Consider how, prior to old age, the combination of both is considered 'normal', and even expected, whereas, in old age, the 'take' aspect tends to be the one that attracts attention and is even used by some to apportion blame.

Almost 30 years ago I was sharing with a colleague my disappointment, as one social worker to another, that the anti-ageist challenge in eldercare was not as strong as I would have hoped. Sensing that I was becoming demoralised, he gave me a copy of a book by Wendy Lustbader (1991), in which she explores the concept of dependency and makes the point that we can sometimes get so drawn into the project of helping (which we perceive as being kind) that we fail to see that this can be perceived by the recipient as reinforcing the dependency that already makes them feel useless and worthless, hence negatively affecting their self-esteem:

> Frail people are generally denied chances to give something back to their helpers or to their communities. Their offers are refused with statements like, 'You don't have to do that. We'll take care of everything.' Helpers mean well, without realizing how urgently people in their care crave a tangible counterbalance to their dependency.
>
> *(p. 29)*

On further reading of some of the practice examples she offers, I began to see that I had sometimes been guilty of unintentionally reinforcing dependency and from that point on I became more sensitised to the part I could play in challenging, rather than reinforcing, dependency by both seeking out creative ways to provide opportunities for people to contribute in ways that suited them and, most importantly, to try always to think about how the eldercare I was involved in is perceived by the recipients of it 'from where they're sitting'.

What stands in the way of dependent older people seeking the opportunity to give as well as receive?

To my mind, two things are particularly significant in this respect. The first, as we have already talked about, is the power of ageist stereotyping to reinforce the assumption that older people either (i) cannot give as well as take or (ii) don't want to give as well as take.

With regards to not wanting to reciprocate, it might be the case that it is a matter of personal choice – that is, that someone might feel that they have earned the right to be 'looked after' without any expectation that they give anything in return. I have no evidence to support this, other than my own very small-scale research, and observations from my own working life in the helping professions, but I suspect that such people are in a minority. You might want to take some time out here to think about whether your own experience reflects this. Another factor, and one which I feel is more likely to account for why some older people don't make it obvious that they want to give something back, is that they don't think they have anything to give, or that what they do have to give back might not be appreciated. This self-deprecation can be the result of a process called *internalised ageism*. This form of ageism is characterised by older people, as a result of being on the receiving end of so many messages, delivered in so many ways, to the effect that they are worthless and that their opinions don't matter, coming to believe these assumptions to be true.

And, because they have internalised these assumptions, it doesn't need anyone to tell them that they shouldn't expect to engage in the give and take that has been part of their lives up to the point at which they started needing care support, because they have already accepted this and resigned themselves to losing the basis on which they had previously built their self-esteem.

Those general assumptions can be seen to feed into something more specific, which is that a number of policies and practices are underpinned by a tendency to be risk averse. We'll look at issues relating to risk in more detail in Chapter 8 but it has some relevance to our discussion of reciprocity here, in that it can get in the way of opportunities to reciprocate being made available, even where a need or desire to reciprocate has been recognised. When we are supporting someone to live the life they want to live, we often face a dilemma. That dilemma is related to a duty to protect that person from harm while also supporting their right to take risks.

You may well have faced this dilemma – it is part and parcel of work in the helping professions – and will have become aware that there are no easy answers. It might make us uncomfortable to see people taking risks, but to try to prevent this at all costs is to risk being *over*protective, something we don't have the right to do, apart from in exceptional circumstances. I have come across many occasions where an older person has expressed a desire to give something back for a service or kindness received but has been told that it is 'too dangerous' – like baking some scones (they might burn themselves in the kitchen) or doing a bit of weeding in communal gardens (they might injure themselves or someone else with a garden tool). Some food for thought: the slight possibility of some harm coming to someone set against the likelihood of that person feeling worthless (and their quality of life being diminished as a consequence) – which is the bigger or more significant risk?

So how can the desire to give something back be facilitated?

I would suggest that the point made above about being risk averse would be a good starting point, in the sense that we can help to facilitate (or at least not get in the way of facilitating) what the older people we support want to engage in, in respect of the give and take of life, even if it might expose them to an element of risk. For example, I once became aware that colleagues of an elderly man who had been a long-standing member of an organisation whose members raised money to support disabled war veterans, had taken the decision to relieve him of his duties as secretary when he became immobilised after a stroke and was living, at that point, in a residential home. He was distraught because he was already facing the challenge of finding new ways to make his damaged brain and body work and had then been faced with what he considered to be a worse challenge – that of being thrown on the scrapheap, as he perceived it. Though it exposed him to an element of risk – that of injuring himself transferring between wheelchair and car in order to get to board meetings, and of being out there in 'the big bad dangerous world' instead of the presumed safe environment of the residential home – practical changes and changes in attitude enabled him to continue attending the meetings. With help from a colleague, and a different computer programme which had a voice recognition facility, he was enabled to remain in his post, and went from strength to strength in his recovery.

I refer above to Lustbader's exploration of dependency and would like to share with you her account of a man who had become unable to speak or write following a stroke and whose wife 'confiscated' his wallet and prevented him from going out into the community because she felt he would be unable to communicate his needs and would therefore be vulnerable. Though her overprotectiveness was coming from a place of love, it was also stifling his enjoyment of life and making rehabilitation almost impossible. However, once it was recognised that his reluctance to engage with life was underpinned by anger at having his 'responsibilities' (in this case, to manage the couple's financial affairs) taken from him, it became possible for progress to be made. Though he remained dependent to a degree, having his wallet taken out of the kitchen drawer and put back in his pocket, restored a sense of 'usefulness' that he had been grieving and the couple were able to devise strategies which allowed him to engage in life beyond their home in a safe and life-affirming way.

Maybe you can think of examples where someone has been enabled to, or prevented from, getting the positive boost to self-esteem that can come from giving something back? That is, where their spiritual wellbeing has been considered alongside their physical wellbeing.

From Where I'm Sitting: Magda's Story

Don't get me wrong, I'm really grateful that I can have help because, without it, I'd be stuck in bed and would probably have starved many times over by now. The only thing I didn't like was having lots of different people coming in all the time. You don't get time to know people and they don't get a chance to get to know you. Anyway, since I mentioned this to my care manager things have got better and most days, a lovely young woman named Kate comes up to my flat to make me some breakfast. I have that in bed while my tablets get to work and then she helps me to get washed and dressed. I'm in a sort of bedsit arrangement – a sort of studio apartment if you want to be posh – and so I can see Kate working in the kitchenette from my bed and recliner in the 'lounge' bit. Don't get me wrong, she does her best, but I had to say something after the umpteenth time she'd made toast for me. 'I quite like toast but can't I have a change please?', I said to her one day 'I'd really prefer something more savoury'. Turned out that toast is all that Kate could 'cook' so that's why I've been having it so often and why she would never ask what I want.

So we came up with a plan. I'd arrange to have the ingredients in and then I'd give her instructions while she did the actual preparation and cooking in the kitchen. She was amazed at how quick and easy to make my breakfast recipes are, and I got to enjoy the variety. She's getting to be quite the breakfast chef these days and has told me that doing this for me has done a lot for her too. She says she feels more confident about buying and cooking fresh ingredients and now knows that her microwave can do more than just reheat the ready meals she always used to buy. It's a great start to my day watching her blossom under my care. I don't feel quite as useless as I used to.

While it might seem obvious, one way to facilitate the desire to give back is to start from where the person is at. That is, to (i) find out, in the first place, *whether* it is important to them that they can give something back. Where something isn't identified as a need, then a response won't follow so enabling people to share what it is that they aspire to can be very enlightening and provide a basis for taking the next steps, which are to (ii) find out what steps *they* think are necessary to help them get where they want to be in terms of feeling 'useful' and (iii) how *they* think that you can help with this.

Another is to embrace creativity – that is, to resist the temptation to do the same thing in the same way just because it's the way it has always been done.

That isn't to say that the 'same old same old' isn't sometimes the best way anyway, and I'm not suggesting change for the sake of it, but sometimes it can pay dividends to think outside of the box, as it were. For example, some planners have had the foresight to site new facilities for nursery provision for young children within, or near to, residential homes for older people, with the expectation that the older residents might benefit from playing a positive role in helping to educate the children with the development of social and other skills.

At a time of their lives when older people are already facing a number of different challenges, I hope you'll agree that it is unfair to add insult to injury by giving them the impression that we don't think they have a useful role in life any more. There is no basis for making that assumption because, however frail a person becomes, there is still potential for them to give something back if that is what they choose to do. A way can always be found if sensitivity to the need, and the will to help, are there.

Exercise 6

Think about one of the ways in which you give something to other people, or to society more broadly. Now consider the following questions:

What positive benefits do you get from this act of giving?

Do you feel that being able to give, or give back, is an important part of your self-image and/or sense of self-worth?

If you were denied the chance to carry on doing this, how might you feel?

Do you think that the older person or people you support are denied opportunities to give back in ways that have the potential to have a positive effect on their self-image and/or sense of self-worth? If not, how might they be enabled to do so, and what part could you play in that?

Over to you ...

What steps can you take to help you always to remember that the older people you support are capable of giving as well as receiving?

CHAPTER 7

The older people you support are likely to be profoundly affected by multiple and cumulative losses

I have referred in the title of this chapter to multiple and cumulative losses. This is to draw attention to the fact that not only is the *number* of likely losses experienced in old age significant in itself, but also that new loss experiences do not erase the pain and distress caused by previous ones, but have the potential to rekindle those earlier emotions. Have you heard people saying, or maybe have thought this yourself, that older people don't grieve deeply, or for long, because they experience so many losses during their later years that they become used to it? Have you thought that maybe this an incorrect assumption – one bolstered by the ageist assumption that older people are no longer 'like the rest of us', in the sense of having feelings? We could look at it in a different way and guess that maybe, rather than the sheer number and regularity of loss experiences making them easy to shrug off as inevitable and inconsequential, the grieving becomes intensified rather than diluted.

This is partly because, as we will explore below, not only do older people lose significant people in their lives to death, they are also likely to experience other types of losses. The significance of these will vary from one person to another but, where they are experienced as significant to an individual, and this significance is not recognised, the effect can be to doubly disadvantage an older person. That is, not only do they have to grieve for somebody or something (which is itself a difficult process) but they then have to take on board the message that the profoundly troubling nature of their loss experiences isn't validated as being important. And, as a consequence of the assumption that their loss experiences aren't validated as important, the help with grieving that other people are routinely offered tends not to be offered to them. So, to the original loss of somebody or something, is added another loss – the recognition that people don't value you

DOI: 10.4324/9781041054481-8

enough to recognise your suffering or want to help you deal with your pain, not just on an emotional level, but also in terms of how it feels in relation to the spiritual dimension we looked at in Chapter 2.

We'll look a little later at some developments in what the theory base of loss has to say, which can help us to appreciate that people don't grieve their losses in a uniform way. But first, let us look at just some of the many aspects of loss that commonly feature in the lives of older people.

Aspects of loss in old age
Bereavement

Although the age range that is socially defined as 'old age' can cover 30 years or more and, at the age of 60, one's death could still be decades away, death still features quite significantly in most older people's lives. As we get older, we are more likely to have relatives, friends and neighbours dying and leaving us to deal with the implications of their going. Indeed, it is often the case that, when older people are in the situation of needing care support, it is because all of their family or network of friends and neighbours have died before them, leaving them with no one to support them. It is not just an issue of practical support, however. Imagine how it might feel to know that all or most of the people who have shared your experience of life with you no longer exist, or do so only in your memories. This would include your favourite actors, singers, authors, sports stars, and so on, as these people would have played a part in your life too, alongside 'real' friends and family. Sometimes having familiarity with something makes it easier to cope with, but it could also be argued that coping with death becomes *harder* to bear in old age, because each experience reinforces the ones that have gone before, bringing back memories and reinforcing some people's experience of old age as being about losses rather than positive change and new experiences.

Of course, there will be a range of responses to a death. For some, experiencing the death of a friend or relative can be unsettling but manageable within that person's coping resources. That is, they grieve for a while but manage to carry on with the usual routine of their lives without too much upset. But for others, every death can be devastating, each new experience reinforcing and adding to the agony of those that have gone before. If we work on the assumption that older people should be used to it and expect everyone to react in the same way, then some people will not get the support or understanding they need.

Loss of status

In some cultures age itself conveys status, but for many it is a time when the stereotype of older people as useless and powerless tends to overshadow people's achievements and abilities. Consider how much you know about the individuals you support. Did they hold positions of power – remember this can be in public life, paid work or at home? How are they likely to be feeling if they no longer have that status? Might their sense of self-worth, and the part this plays in maintaining their self-esteem, be taking a blow?

Loss of independence

Some individuals will have experienced significant levels of dependency throughout their adult lives (those with disabilities, for example), but many will have been used to deciding what to do, and how and when to do it, by themselves. The increased likelihood of becoming physically frail, or developing dementia, in old age means that quite a lot of older people lose a certain amount of independence. But even though the *means* to be independent may be lost, the *desire* to remain independent is not necessarily lost along with them. Offers to help someone who has lost their independence may be well meant but can have the effect of reinforcing the sense of loss felt at not being able to do things for oneself anymore.

Loss of income

Being old does not necessarily mean being poor, although, for many older people, poverty becomes a very real part of their lives, even if it had not been so before. Loss of earning power, and all the rewards that go with it, can be a loss of significant proportions. Having the financial means to enjoy life and to be able to sort out any unforeseen problems that might arise (household repairs, for example) can lead to a feeling of security, but for those who have been unable to save for such eventualities, old age can be a time where feelings of vulnerability and powerlessness come to the fore.

Loss of home and neighbourhood

Having a place to call one's own is very important to most people. It need not necessarily be a house. For some, home is a room, part of a room, or even a cardboard box or tent that has been personalised. It doesn't necessarily have to be owned, but is somewhere we can identify with and keep private if we so choose. It is our 'own' place. When a home has to be given up, the loss can be very profoundly felt. It is not just a loss of bricks and mortar, but of everything that having a home signifies, such as independent living, being part of a neighbourhood, having control over who enters the property and so on. But it is not just those who enter residential care who can feel a sense of loss in relation to their home. For those dependent older people who are supported in the community, having carers entering their homes can also highlight other forms of loss, including those of privacy and control.

Loss of spontaneity

Think about how many times in the day you decide that you want to have or do something and just get up out of the chair and make it happen. For some older people who are limited in ability or opportunity 'just making it happen' may not be so easy. A lack of opportunity for spontaneity can also be a feature of older people's lives if they spend long periods of time in hospital or live in residential settings where meals and snacks are provided by other people and according to fixed schedules. Some people are provided with an opportunity to make themselves, or their visitors, a drink or snack as and when the fancy takes them, but many are not given the means to do so, even where they have the ability.

Though I have presented these as a list of potential losses, it has to be appreciated that these tend not to be experienced in isolation. Typically, people experience a combination of the above, and more besides.

Many older people will tell you that old age is a very liberating and positive time of life. However, it is important to remember that, for many, it is a time when loss features very significantly in their lives, but is felt no less deeply than at any other life stage. If the staff who become involved in these people's lives are unaware (or aware but dismissive) of loss issues and the emotional impact they can have, then they run the risk of harming people in their attempts to help them. So how can we learn more?

From Where I'm Sitting: Glen's Story

I'm very fond of Jacinta. She's been more like a sister than a care worker, what with supporting me through all that's been going on in my life over the past few years but I sometimes wish she wasn't always so flipping cheerful! She always seems to be looking for a positive slant on things, but sometimes it isn't what I want to do. Take last summer. I'd been looking after Dad for so long – never expected him to live to be over a hundred – and me just had my eightieth. When he died everyone said it was a blessing but it didn't feel like that to me. Yes, it was hard sometimes, but having him around for all that time was lovely too and some people don't get that chance.

I'd always had him in my life and then there he was, gone. I didn't expect to miss him so much, but there you are, I do. I'd have given anything for him to have been at my birthday party but there was hardly even a mention of him. Perhaps they thought it wouldn't be 'appropriate' but to me it felt like a kick in the teeth. 'Enjoy yourself while you still can'– that's what Jacinta kept saying – 'you've got a new lease of life now'. And perhaps she's right in a way, but sometimes I just don't feel like 'celebrating' his going. Seems disrespectful to me.

I was having a bit of a think about this the other day. I'd read in the paper about a lad who'd died a few days short of his eighteenth birthday and how his family had said how much easier it had been to tell people on social media about the party being cancelled than having to do it by phone. And I felt so sorry for them – especially his younger brother – because that must have been so awful. So why did people not think to cancel or postpone my party? I was grieving, for goodness' sake, and why *shouldn't I have been. I wish I'd had the energy to cancel the party myself, but then I might have felt worse because everyone was just trying to cheer me up. As it was, it felt like another ordeal. On reflection, I suppose I'm just a bit disappointed that the people I thought know me well don't really. Perhaps what I'm really struggling with is the increasing realisation that this might be a taste of things to come – like my feelings won't matter to people?*

Developing our understanding

Many people continue to assume that bereavement is about people working their way through 'stages', such as shock, denial, acceptance and so on, even though developments in loss theory over the past 20 years or more have challenged this assumption as being unhelpful. Let's look at three more recent, and well-accepted, models of grieving.

Dual process theory

This is an approach developed by Stroebe and Schut (Thompson, 2022). They suggest that, rather than working through one stage before moving on to the next, people who have been bereaved jump backwards and forwards between two phases, or what they refer to as 'orientations'. This shift can happen at any time, even within the space of a day. For example, if you are grieving, it is possible to feel positive about the future in the morning and yet, by the afternoon, something might have reminded you about the person you are grieving for and you feel that you can't go on without them. By the evening of that same day, after sitting alone in your garden with your memories for a few hours, you might get back to feeling that the future has a purpose again. Initially, according to this model, in the 'loss orientation' phase we focus more often on what or who we have lost, but in the 'restoration orientation' phase we are able to focus more readily on the future – not to leave

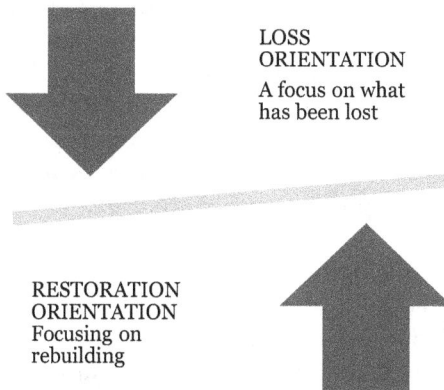

LOSS
ORIENTATION
A focus on what
has been lost

RESTORATION
ORIENTATION
Focusing on
rebuilding

Figure 7.1 Dual process theory

who we have lost behind, but to envisage a future of some sort. We will probably experience the first aspect more often in the early days of bereavement, and the second aspect more often later on, but the point being made is that we will still tend to move between the two at any given time, and can be 'catapulted' back into a loss orientation even decades after a loss has occurred, perhaps by seeing a photograph or thinking of someone on a date that has particular significance, like a birthday.

Thinking about bereavement from this perspective reminds us that we shouldn't base our judgements about how someone is coping with a loss from just one visit — the impression we get might not give us a true picture. For example, we may be unaware of a special memory, or anniversary that might be triggering a move from one orientation to the other. Without bothering to get the true picture the potential to badly misread a situation, and respond insensitively, is high.

Meaning-reconstruction theory

Another challenge to the 'stages' approach comes from the work of Neimeyer and Sands (2011) who remind us that, to understand how people grieve, we must take into account their meaning making – that is, the unique way in which they are trying to make sense of their loss experience and what it means to them. For example, what is experienced as a traumatic loss for one person, might not be so for another. To the family of a terminally ill 95-year-old man whose pain cannot be managed very well and who is experiencing frightening hallucinations, death might be welcomed and grief experienced differently than by the family of a healthy 17-year-old killed when out driving his new car for the first time. People are often ridiculed for grieving the loss of a pet more than the loss of a person but, for some people, it might be that the pet had meant more to them than any person ever had. For example, if a pet cat or dog or horse is what has helped someone through the difficult times in their life by providing a constant supply of unconditional love, then to lose that pet can be a very significant form of bereavement and more so, perhaps, than the death of a human relative who had not featured in their life very much.

From this perspective, grieving is not about 'recovering' as it is not possible to return to the old 'normality' – how things were before the loss. Instead, grieving is said to involve the constructing of a new 'normality'. That is, reconstructing what your life means to you without the person or thing you have lost. Things will never be exactly the same again but, in time, it will be possible to see life as whole again: a different whole, but an acceptable one nevertheless. Explaining loss in this way, with reference to what a loss *means* to someone, helps us to appreciate that making spot judgements about people's reactions to loss can be very misguided.

The continuing bonds thesis

It is often assumed that the ultimate aim of grief 'work', in whatever form that might take, is to 'get over' a loss and to 'move on'. I have known many bereaved people who live in fear of losing their connection with a loved one (and that others might forget them too, when they die). For that reason they might engage in rituals that signify that they are not disrespecting the relationship that they once had with someone or something – setting a place at the table for them when the family gather to celebrate an important event or festive occasion, for example. Or talking to them while out on what had been a favourite walk of theirs, even though they are not physically present. Klass, Silverman and Nickman (1996) challenged the expectation that bereaved people should move on, suggesting that maintaining bonds is a healthy and helpful way to grieve, rather than a dysfunctional one. In a similar vein to meaning-reconstruction theory, the continuing bonds thesis has as its premise that death need not end a relationship if new ways can be found to have that relationship continue in meaningful ways. Death changes a relationship but doesn't end it but this isn't always taken on board and some people might feel uncomfortable if a bereaved person chooses to continue and perhaps modify the bonds they have upheld, rather than break them and, as a consequence, try to persuade them to 'move on'. If this is the case, then it begs the question 'whose needs are we trying to meet here'?

What do you think about these perspectives on grieving? Do you think that they are helpful for making sense of what happens when people are having to deal with a significant loss, or series of losses, and therefore for how you might be able to help them?

TIP! Try not to put loss and grief issues to the back of your mind because they are difficult to deal with. Awareness and sensitivity are often all that the older people you support will ask of you.

A chance to say goodbye

While things are hopefully improving in this respect, one group of people who are sometimes still treated insensitively when a death occurs in a residential environment or hospital is the remaining residents or patients. Thankfully, this situation is being increasingly recognised as one that needs managing sensitively, perhaps through the use of rituals, but it is still the case that deaths are sometimes 'hushed up' and bodies removed secretly from the building. No doubt the intention is to protect people from becoming distressed, but does this show respect for the person who has died or for the feelings of those who remain? If you work with people in a communal home, think about how death and dying are dealt with there. Is there, for example, an opportunity to mark the death in some way? We're back to the meaning making referred to earlier, in the sense that however small the gesture is, it shows others that the person was valued in life. To not mark their death in any way suggests to those who are left that they didn't really matter. Imagine how it might feel to know that you might die and no one thinks it worthy of note or commemoration. Writing something in a book of remembrance, or stopping to look at a photograph or keepsake can help people to come to terms with a death, and feel that their own deaths will be marked in a similar way.

Many people find rituals helpful when grieving a loss, but this isn't always appreciated by others, especially when the loss isn't death related. For example, many who have to give up their homes experience a very profound sense of loss because it signifies to them that, while they might gain in some ways, they are giving up an awful lot too. Even when there are advantages to the move, it can still be distressing or even traumatic, as it involves breaking ties with the past, as well as getting used to new surroundings. So, for example, finding some way to mark that transition, a ritualised 'goodbye' through the use of photographs or keepsakes, or by transplanting favourite plants into pots in the garden of their new home, for example, can sometimes help to make the transition less difficult.

In conclusion, in this chapter we have explored a number of important issues. In particular, we have noted that:

- Loss is likely to feature significantly in older people's lives but familiarity with it doesn't necessarily make it easier to deal with.
- Many losses will be death related, but there will also be many that are unconnected with death, and these can be devastating too.
- If we are not sensitive to the fact that an older person is grieving, we may do them considerable harm without realising it.
- Different people grieve in different ways. As there is no set or standard way of grieving, there is no set or standard way of helping.
- We cannot take the pain of grief away but we can ask a grieving person how best we might help them in their particular set of circumstances.

Grieving is not an easy process, and it can be difficult to know how to help a grieving person because of the uniqueness of their loss, their personality and their coping strategies. But maybe remembering, and respecting, that uniqueness is a good starting point.

Exercise 7

Thinking about one of the people you support, make a list of all of the losses, or aspects of loss, that you know or suspect they have experienced, or are experiencing, in their old age. Once you have made the list, go through it and, for each loss experience or potential loss experience that you have identified, think about whether that experience has been recognised by others and validated as significant. If you have identified one or more that haven't been, why do you think that might have been the case?

If you have found this exercise thought-provoking and useful, you could repeat the process for other people that you support. If you notice patterns emerging, why might this be the case?

Over to you ...

What steps can you take to help you always to remember that the older people you support are likely to be profoundly affected by multiple and cumulative losses?

CHAPTER 8

The older people you support are entitled to take risks that you and others may not think are in their best interests

Risk taking

There's no getting away from the fact that life is all about taking risks. Without engaging in risk taking we would never get out of bed, or leave the house. And that's what we're talking about here – those everyday risks, rather than the ones some thrill seekers engage in, like tightrope walking between two skyscrapers, or leaping off the sides of mountains with what seems like very little in the way of assistance or protection. Getting out of bed and going about our day-to-day business might seem very tame in comparison, but involves risk nevertheless. We could, for example, trip over something and knock ourselves out on a piece of furniture, or slip on a wet floor in the bathroom and do a lot of damage to fixtures and fittings as well as ourselves. I know several people who have found out the hard way how sharp broken porcelain is and how difficult it can be to get up when wedged into a tight space after a fall. And then there's the matter of getting some breakfast. It seems that household kitchens are dangerous places. We could electrocute ourselves, scald ourselves, choke on our food, cut ourselves on sharp implements – and that's just for starters. Things might get even riskier if we throw into the mix the fact that we might not be fully awake and therefore more likely to make mistakes, or we might be rushing around and both literally and metaphorically cutting corners. And that's before we even leave the house!

If we get into a car and start driving, we engage in the risky business of moving a huge chunk of metal around public spaces, while negotiating other people doing the same, and avoiding those people who are out doing their own risk taking by walking and negotiating the various hazards they might face, as well as managing the possibility that they might get heatstroke or hypothermia if they don't manage the risks associated with dressing appropriately for the prevailing

DOI: 10.4324/9781041054481-9

weather conditions. It might seem like I'm labouring the point a bit, but the issue is that we tend to take such risks in our stride, if we recognise them as risks at all. Unless they're brought into sharp focus for some reason (like actually having one of those accidents in the kitchen) most of us probably don't consider ourselves to live particularly risky lives, even though daily life is fraught with dangers. We just get on with things and make our own minds up whether to take notice of advice that we're given – on the dangers of smoking, for example.

So, imagine if someone were to tell you that risk taking is no longer allowed. That is, if you survive the night without being accidentally suffocated by your pillow, or electrocuted while turning your bedside light on, you are not allowed to get out of bed unless you first put on a protective padded suit in case you fall, and a pair of insulated gloves and rubber-soled shoes before you touch anything which involves electricity. And as for anything involving water, just don't go there!

This might all seem a bit ridiculous, but it's just to remind us that we all take risks in our daily lives, even if they're not big ones, or even conscious ones, and we take it as read that, unless we don't have the mental capacity to understand risk, we *can* take those risks because we have the right to. But it is often the experience of older people, especially those who have some degree of frailty, that the right to take risks is denied them, or that they are persuaded to minimise those risks in ways that result in what they might experience as 'diminished lives'. The vast majority of workers who support older people would want them to come to no harm but we have to take care to ensure that the power to define what constitutes 'harm', and indeed 'risk', does not rest with one individual or one profession, but is open to debate between all people involved in the management of someone's care, which includes, of course, the older person him- or herself. This is because, despite assumptions to the contrary, unless a person has had their right to make their own judgements about risk taking taken away because they are deemed to lack the mental capacity to make those judgements, the final word on the matter rests with him or her, however uncomfortable this might be for worried relatives, friends and support workers. So, if we can't take risk away, can we help manage it in ways that don't contravene the right to take risks?

From Where I'm Sitting: Alice's Story

If one more person comes here and tells me how dangerous my stairs are I think I'll get the locks changed to keep any more out. Yes, I'm well aware that I'm not getting any younger and I'm well aware that those stairs are very steep but I was born in this cottage and I've been going up and down those stairs for eighty-something years now so I think I've got the measure of them. In all those years I've only fallen down them twice. The first time was when I was in my forties and tried to carry too many books up there at one go. Didn't half hurt my back, but the doctor said nothing was broken and left it at that. I told myself to be more careful in future but you don't, do you!

Such a hoo-hah the second time though, which was a few months ago when I missed my footing on the carpet and didn't manage to grab the handrail in time. Hurt more than my pride – I had a bruise on my hip like you wouldn't believe – but I didn't break anything. Wish I hadn't been to the surgery about it now because there's been one after another telling me I should have a stairlift or else move to a bungalow or a care home even. Why on earth would I want all that hassle? If I was falling down the stairs every other day I could understand it, but really, what's all the fuss about? I felt a bit shaky for a few days so I slept on the sofa for a couple of nights – no different from what I've always done since a child if I've not felt well. I'd rather sleep in my bed upstairs though so that's what I've gone back to and I'll hear no more about it thank you. They can go and worry about somebody that needs worrying about. I thought they'd be happy now that I've taken the carpet up and had non-slip treads put on the stairs but every time someone comes they still say that I shouldn't go up them because they're steep. Well I've got news for them – I can and I will.

Some things to consider

- The need to be clear about what we mean, or questioning what other people mean, when we/they describe an older person as being 'at risk'. At risk of what? Of dying? Of injuring themselves or others? Of being injured or neglected by others? Of being harassed? Of being socially isolated? Of being ignored? Of being financially abused or robbed by online scammers or burglars? Clarifying the specific nature of the risk allows for targeted responses that can help people to live their preferred lifestyles for as long as they can. Attempting to remove all and every aspect of risk is not only impossible, but is likely to be experienced as oppressive.

- Knowing the nature of the risk is helpful, but what about the severity or perceived severity? What implications might there be if the risk isn't removed or managed? And is there agreement on the perception of what a good outcome would be? For example, is the person in question *actually* at risk of harm at a specific point in time, or is there just a *possibility* that some harm might come to them in some form at some time? Is there a possibility that a proposed programme of risk management aimed at protecting someone could constitute *over*protection, and therefore an infringement of their rights?

- Is the risk always present or just in particular circumstances? For example, is someone who lives alone and is prone to debilitating anxiety attacks subject to them at all times of the day or night, regardless of other factors, or only when his friendly neighbour is not at home? And is the woman who is at risk of financial exploitation by her nephew always in this position or only when circumstances allow for him to visit without others in the family being aware?

■ Whose definition of risk are people working to? You might notice that some people's assessments of risk carry more weight than others and are less likely than others to be called into question. The power to 'call the shots' may well be connected to professional status. If there is a disagreement about risk management, how is this resolved and what protocols are in place, if any, to allow for the person deemed to be 'at risk' to have their perspective heard or represented?

■ Is there a possibility that removing or reducing one form of risk can allow other forms to be introduced? For example, if a frail older person lives alone it seems fair to say that persuading them to move into a more supported living facility might reduce the risk of physical harm if they are prone to falls because there would presumably be more assistance available to help with getting around the place more safely. However, it has the potential to *increase* the risk of psychological and spiritual harm if they perceive the lifestyle choice they have been persuaded to make as one that has a negative effect on their sense of self and place in the world.

I remember reading in a magazine some time ago about how, in one of the Scandinavian countries, some older people with dementia who lived in a particular group setting were encouraged to go swimming (without supervision) in the

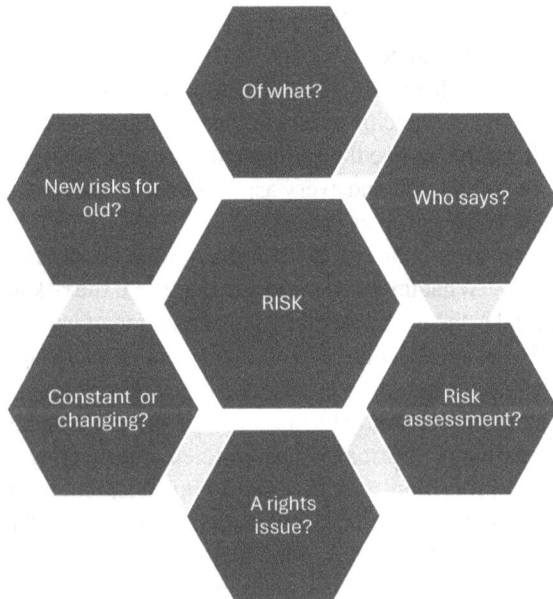

Figure 8.1 Risk analysis

nearby lake if they wanted to. As this was something that most of them would have been used to doing on a regular basis throughout the course of their lives, and without coming to any harm, those supporting them deemed the potential (and seemingly low) risk of them coming to harm to be of less significance than the risk of them suffering in other ways because of a reduction in their quality of life. Food for thought there, I think you'll agree.

If you hear or read about someone being 'at risk' don't take that comment at face value. Ask questions which will give you a better understanding of the nature and degree of the risk and who identified it as a problem.

The discussion in this chapter has probably raised more questions than answers, but that should serve to remind us that risk management is not an exact science – there is never going to be a formula that will tell us what the right thing to do is because every set of circumstances will be different and, because we are people working with people, every set of working relationships will be different. We can only do our best to ensure that, if the older people we support *are* denied the chance to take risks, it is because there is evidence to support the case that their ability to understand the consequences of those choices is impaired or lacking for some reason, and not just because they are old and assumed to need protecting from themselves on that basis.

Care workers are well placed to help ensure that risk management is informed by risk assessment in order to help ensure that questions such as those we have explored above are asked – because they are often the people who spend most time with the older people in question. We can all look to our own practice to ensure that it is based on anti-ageist and rights-based principles, but we can also help others to do the same by flagging up situations where we feel that people's rights to take risks are, or might be, being overshadowed by other considerations. And if we're not sure about what these are, we can ask. Let's keep anti-ageist practice on the agenda. There's no denying that many older people *do* need protecting from risks and that risk management needs to be taken very seriously. But so too does the potential for *over*protective policies and practices to undermine people's rights when there is no justification other than their age and other people's ageist assumptions.

Exercise 8

Have you ever been in a situation where an older person you support is making a choice or choices that you don't think is or are in their best interests? If you can't think of one, for the purposes of this exercise, imagine that someone is choosing to continue drinking large amounts of alcohol on a daily basis, against medical advice, and that they often ask you to buy it for them on your way to visit:

Do you feel that the person in question had or has the right to make their own lifestyle choices? Does their age make a difference to your judgement on this? Should it?

Do you feel that anyone else has the right to take that autonomy away from them? If so, in what circumstances? Who has the right to decide what a person's best interests are?

What might you be able to do, in line with your duty to protect vulnerable adults, to dissuade him or her from making choices that are not in their best interests, as you see them?

If you are experiencing a dilemma about risk management and your part in it, who could you go to for advice?

Over to you ...

What steps can you take to help you always to remember that the older people you support are entitled to take risks that you and/or others might not think are in their best interests?

CHAPTER 9

The older people you support are partners in their care arrangements

When we're thinking about older people being partners in the arranging of the support they receive, we need to be clear about what partnership working means and to understand that it operates at a number of levels, as we'll see below. But the starting point has to be that there should be no justification for leaving older people out of discussions which are about them and their current and future lives. If we do, we are saying that the older person's perspective is not important, and that it is therefore acceptable at both policy and practice levels to 'do to' older people, rather than to 'work with' them when responding to their care needs. I'm sure you'll agree that the latter premise is a much more respectful one and, where it feeds into policy and practice, dignified care is more likely to be the outcome. Unfortunately, things can get in the way of effective partnership working, and we'll look at these but, first, let's explore the term a bit more.

What do we mean by partnership?

The term 'partnership' is often used to describe working relationships between a number of different agencies. We can see partnership arrangements operating, for example, in situations where social workers and police officers work together to address child protection issues. Another example would be when information and expertise are shared between agencies (housing, law enforcement, drug and alcohol rehabilitation, and so on) towards a shared goal relating to homelessness. With regard to the work you do as a social care worker to support older people, the most likely partnership you will witness, or be part of, is that between health and social care agencies, though that is not to say that other working partnerships will not come into the picture. Many of the people you support will need that

DOI: 10.4324/9781041054481-10

support because of frailty associated with ageing and the increased likelihood of illness and disability that accompanies it. It might be the case, therefore, that the care you provide is part of a package of support that is provided by a number of agencies, and perhaps even more than one department within those agencies. So, for example, one person might be supported by representatives from community nursing, social work, one or more domiciliary agencies, physiotherapy providers and debt advice workers, to name but a few.

Sometimes the partnership aspect of the support provided to a particular person is part of an explicit agreement to work within that model, with someone being designated to take on the role of coordinator to ensure that everyone is 'singing from the same hymn sheet' as it were – that is, to help ensure that everyone is working to an agreed set of aims and objectives relating to a person's needs, and 'best interests', whatever they are perceived to be. Sometimes, less formal partnership arrangements can work well, but if there is no clarity about aims and objectives, a situation can arise where potentially helpful outcomes are not realised because people and programmes work against, rather than with, each other.

So, partnerships can be formal or informal, planned, or the unplanned coming together of involved parties, successfully or otherwise. As we have seen, partnerships can operate at the level of practice, as individual workers go about the business of supporting individual older people. But they operate at other levels too, such as that of policymaking. People, or groups of people, will be working in partnership within and across organisations (the one which employs you, local authorities, health boards, government departments and so on) with the aim of agreeing on things such as standards, provision, monitoring and funding, to name but some of the aspects of eldercare which need addressing if the older people who need support are to get that support. All good stuff, we might say – key people and agencies working together to achieve a good outcome for older people with support needs, but who counts as key and who decides what a good outcome is? While it is increasingly the case these days that the older people themselves – arguably the people best placed to be key partners in decision making because they know what a good outcome feels like from where they are sitting – are finding ways to have their voices heard, this does not always happen.

Co-production

In this respect, you may have come across the term 'co-production' or be involved in co-production initiatives. It is a relatively new policy initiative and so it is possible that you may not be aware of it. As a concept and aspiration co-production was identified in an evaluation (by users of support services and their carers) of the Social Services and Well-being (Wales) Act 2014 as a means to challenge the power imbalance that can be seen to exist between providers of support services and those (including their carers) who use them. In essence, it is about giving those people a say in how services are designed and delivered – a voice. Waters

(2023), herself a user of several public services, makes a very valid point about how a power imbalance between professionals and 'ordinary' people can feel:

> We all use services, every single one of us, so all are service users. For example, when you go to see a medic or arrange something for a family member, think about how that feels. What emotional response do you have when you realise you are not being listened to, your concerns have been diminished and what you need has been dismissed? That is a power imbalance and we have all felt it or seen it play out at some point. Consider how much easier this becomes when there is respectful engagement, when you feel like an equal. If there is transparency and mutual regard it just makes life easier.
>
> *(p. 72)*

And maybe you'd agree that it makes things easier because its fairer – life shouldn't have to be a struggle to get a sense of control over what is made available to someone and how it is delivered but this situation will persist unless the insights that service users and their carers bring to the table are given at least an element of credibility, if not equal credibility, as a source of expertise. And that is what is at the core of co-production – breaking down the assumption that professionals 'know best', thereby reflecting the importance of partnership as a key social care value.

From Where I'm Sitting: Erik's Story

I'm Erik. All my life I've had painful joints because of a condition I've had since childhood. I've learned to make the best of things, and live within my limits, but I've also tried to do as much as I can for myself. I know what helps and what makes me feel worse and so I've tried to make life as comfortable as I can by keeping to routines. That way I feel more in control of my life. I've never had a lot of money to splash around, but one luxury I try to give myself is warmth. If I can keep warm then the pain is kept down – it can become unbearable, so I do everything I can not to get cold.

If I have a soak in my bath every morning, it helps set me up for the day and then another soak before bedtime relaxes me enough to let me get at least some sleep. It might sound like a luxury, but it's the only way I can keep going. I wonder how much longer I'll be able to manage. My baths are a necessity for me – as essential to me as a holiday is to my son, and I've given up other things to be able to afford them. I even spent my savings on a special bath, which I managed to use on my own until recently.

Now, even that has got too difficult so I'm having people calling in to help me. But that's the problem. You see, they think they're helping me, but they're not really. Take yesterday, for example. I'd had a bad night and my joints were throbbing with pain. What kept me going in the small hours was the thought that I'd be in that soothing water before much longer. But, when the carer arrived he made my breakfast and offered me help with washing myself down and getting dressed. He said he was particularly rushed that morning and anyway, why did I need a bath when I'd only just had one the night before? There are three different carers who call and they all seem to miss the point. I like to keep clean, but there's more to it than that. If they've only got a certain amount of time, then why do they insist on doing what I don't need and never asked for when it deprives me of what I do need? It doesn't work for me, and it's a waste of time and money into the bargain. Who are they to know what's best for me?

So, what might get in the way of older people being considered as partners in care planning?

There are a number of issues we could cover here if space permitted but I suggest we focus on just four to get the thought processes going. Feel free, though, to make your own notes if these points spark off other ideas or lines of thought.

Assumptions about what counts as expertise

When a number of parties come together to work on a problem, the likelihood is that there will be a number of different perspectives on the exact nature of the problem and on how to address it. That can be a good thing because the sharing of expertise can throw light on things in ways which might not have happened otherwise. In an ideal situation, each party would have an equal chance to have their opinion +heard and respected but unfortunately this doesn't always happen because some forms of expertise attract more respect than others. For example, if you work in a hospital, or have been a patient in one, have you noticed that there is often a degree of deference to those representing the medical profession?

It may be that this is in the process of changing, as the expertise of nurse practitioners and highly trained practitioners in other fields is drawn on where a team approach is favoured. However, even where this is the case, expertise is still often seen as something that only results from years of training and experience in a particular field or subject, letters after your name, and so on. But expertise exists in other forms, as service user involvement initiatives have highlighted. For example, a doctor will have expertise in the disease processes relating to osteoarthritis, and a physiotherapist will have expertise in rehabilitating someone affected by osteoarthritis so that they have the fullest possible range of movement within the limits of their condition. But the person who is *living* the condition and its consequences has expertise too. Without feedback from the 'insider' perspective, any attempts to treat or alleviate the condition, or support someone to live with it, will largely be based on guesswork – a best estimate, as it were. That expertise is part and parcel of every process of care planning, there to be drawn on to help ensure that unique problems are addressed by solutions that are appropriate for a particular individual and their particular set of circumstances. If that 'insider' perspective is not recognised as expertise in its own right, as proponents of a co-production approach would argue, then this is one of the factors that can get in the way of inclusive partnership working.

Assumptions about a person's capacity to engage in partnership working

If we think back to the (wrong and unhelpful) ageist stereotype of incompetence – that to be old is to be decrepit, useless, and so on – then another factor that can get in the way of older people being involved as partners in the planning of their care is the assumption that they are not up to it for one reason or another. These could include the assumption that they lack the understanding or confidence (or both) to participate but, even if this were the case, it would not justify their being seen as observers from the sidelines, rather than players on the field. If the will is there to involve them as partners in the process, then ways can be found to facilitate that. For example, where confidence is low, having a friend or advocate to assist or represent them could promote their inclusion, as too would a commitment to the avoidance of the jargon that the professional workers in partnerships are likely to understand, but which excludes the very people who should be at the centre of discussions. Take some time out here to reflect on other ways that someone who is unconfident or intellectually impaired could be enabled to participate.

Assumptions about a person's desire to engage in partnership working

In previous sections we have given some thought to how internalised ageism may contribute to an element of unwillingness to be involved. Some older people, for example, might feel that they don't have a right to a say in how things go, and should just be grateful for what's on offer. Where this is left unchallenged, it condones the policy and practice of service-led provision of support. That is, where a range of support services is offered and the only options available are to take it or leave it. Where there is a meaningful commitment to including older people as partners in the design and provision of the support they receive, this promotes the person-centred care model which should allow for unique problems to be addressed in unique ways.

A lack of commitment to making partnership possible

We are talking here about creating opportunities or overcoming obstacles. If, in theory, an older person is considered to be entitled to be a partner in the planning of their care, but the opportunity for them to do so does not exist, or is not created, then I'm sure you'll agree that this theoretical entitlement is tokenistic – just people paying lip service to an entitlement, rather than making it happen. Consider, for example, that if multi-disciplinary discussions about someone's care takes place in someone's office, then it is likely to be difficult (and costly) for the older person in question to be part of that group. Holding such meetings in the person's own home would be one way to address what amounts to a power imbalance, as would setting up an online facility for them, and others, to participate in real time without being physically present.

> **TIP!** If you have ever felt affronted by someone making a decision on your behalf without giving you the opportunity to be part of the discussion that led up to it, remember that feeling and let it alert you to how an older person you support might be feeling if that happens to them.

What part can you play in overcoming these obstacles?

So, what can you do to help ensure that your practice, as far as is possible, respects and promotes the idea that 'working with' not 'doing to' is the right thing to do? The following points might provide food for thought:

- Work from a mindset that challenges the notion that there are older people who need care and support and there are people who do the supporting and know what's best for the older people because that's their job. Might not strategies based on a 'we'll work on your problems together' model allow for a more inclusive outcome for the older people involved?

- Remember that effective communication is a key component of inclusive partnership working. Do effective channels of communication exist where you work? What counts as effective? For example, do the older people in question have the opportunity to have their perspective heard in a medium with which they are familiar – in their preferred language, for example? And, if it is heard, is it understood and respected? Is it recorded anywhere, for example? And, most importantly, is it acted on?

- Don't be complacent or allow others to be. How do you know whether someone you support is happy with the support they are receiving? Are the arrangements reviewed and evaluated? Do those on the receiving end play a meaningful part in the partnership process that would be respectful of their expertise?

- Help to promote the creative thinking that can overcome barriers. For example, developments in technology mean that people don't even need to be in the same physical space to operate as partners, and can provide innovative ways to aid communication. But this all has to start with awareness and acceptance of the premise that we should work towards a desired end *with* the people we support, rather than merely 'do to' them. Working in partnership *with* people is to treat them as people. Doing *to* them is to treat them as things.

What is your experience of partnership working? Does it include or exclude the older people concerned? Maybe you've seen evidence of inclusive partnership in action – in people's own homes or through the medium of virtual technologies perhaps? The opportunity to participate on an equal footing with others in the partnership, and with respect for the older person's expertise, may be difficult to put into practice but that should not justify a policy of not bothering to try which, in my experience, is not uncommon. I hope that your experience is more positive but, if not, be inspired to come up with some creative thinking that will take things in a better direction.

Exercise 9

Thinking about your own life and its challenges, and using health and health-care as an example, ask yourself the following questions:

In what ways do I ensure that when any decisions are made that relate to my health (define health as broadly as you want to) they are made *by* me and not *for* me? List as many as you can.

Do you think that, when older people become frail and need help from others, the same range of options and strategies that you have listed above are open to them too? If not, why might that be?

What can you do to help address any issues you have identified above? Remember that it is not your responsibility alone, so this could include flagging things up to managers or helping an older person to.

Over to you ...
What steps can you take to help you always to remember that the older people you support are partners in their care?

The older people you support are possibly facing many different challenges

As you'll be aware if you've been working through this manual from the beginning, we've already looked at some of the many ways in which old age can be a challenge, and also how this can be compounded by the fact that the extent and degree of those challenges can often be overlooked or minimised. While we've focused, this far, on particular aspects, we've also noted that they aren't experienced in isolation. Life is complex and messy and it would be a lot easier to deal with our problems if they queued up and waited in an orderly line until we could deal with one challenge before moving on to tackle the next.

In this chapter, as a way of summarising the work you've done this far, and to further draw out the implications of that work, we'll focus on how it is often the case that old age brings multiple, and interrelated, challenges. That's not to paint an unduly negative picture of old age – many people enjoy this life stage immensely, despite the challenges it brings – but we would do well to bear in mind that it can take a lot of energy and resilience to keep on batting back the curved balls that life keeps throwing at us, and it can feel tempting to just lie down on the other side of the net and wave the white flag while being pelted with more balls. As the saying goes, 'old age isn't for the faint hearted'.

We'll spend some time thinking about resilience and how we can help promote it, but first let's consider how it might feel to be facing a combination of different challenges associated with the experiencing of old age, any one of which has the potential to be significant, or even overwhelming, even on its own. Let's remind ourselves of some of them:

DOI: 10.4324/9781041054481-11

Being expected to live up (or down) to the negative stereotype of old age

Despite campaigns against ageism, the negative stereotype of old age continues to be a powerful one. We see this in the fact that 'ordinary' achievements are highlighted as something extraordinary, purely because the person doing the achieving is an older person – the implication being that older people aren't expected to achieve anything much. We see it too in the way that old age is typically portrayed as a time of loss, impairment and stagnation – and, worse still, that it is acceptable to make fun of older people on that basis – when it is so often a time of personal development, learning and growth, rather than decline. Where the 'background music' (those messages that they hear from many different quarters, and time and time again) to people's lives reflects negativity rather than positivity, it is not surprising that many older people fall into the trap of believing other people's perceptions to be the truth – the reality of their lives – rather than merely one perception amongst many. And, where those perceptions reflect low expectations, this can contribute to older people having low expectations of themselves too, and tailoring their lives accordingly (the internalised discrimination we talked about earlier). That is, they try to live their lives according to other people's perceptions of how they *should* live their lives, rather than how they would *like* to live them.

Do you think that you are in a position to help those older people who are living down to the negative stereotype to challenge, rather than accept it? If so, how? If not, what might be getting in the way? For example, is the culture of being risk averse that we discussed earlier having an impact in your work settings, on the choices people are able to make and on your role too?

Having to face being treated as just another old person, rather than as an individual

We hear a lot about promoting dignity in eldercare, and rightly so. You can probably bring to mind lots of situations where dignity can be compromised – being dressed in someone else's clothes, or referred to by the wrong name, for example. Such examples can be seen to be underpinned by a lack of respect for personhood – that mix of aspects which makes a person *the* person that they are, and not any other person. Promoting dignity is something we should be able to work out from how we expect to be treated by other people. If our dignity is compromised for some reason, it can be a horrible experience and something which we would not like others to experience if we are genuinely committed to promoting good quality eldercare. Do we not expect to be respected as the unique person we are, for what it is that makes us, us and not a clone of someone else? And, if that is the case, then why wouldn't we expect it to be important to the older people we support too?

TIP! It is not uncommon for an older person who is experiencing difficulties to explain them away by saying 'it's just because I'm old'. If you hear that, use it as a prompt to explore whether it is 'just about being old' because the likelihood is that it is not.

How we as individuals support those that we do can have a huge impact on the extent to which their sense of self as important and valued people is maintained, and it is to be hoped that our actions as individual workers help to that end.

However, it is a big ask for the problem to be solved by individual practice alone, however good that practice is, because the de-individualising (and therefore de-personalising) of older people are manifestations of ageism operating at a broader level – that is, one whereby it is deemed acceptable in a culture for these processes to continue unchallenged. Consider, for example, whether more attention is paid to differences *between* generations (that is, what life stage a person is at, and on expectations relating to that) than on differences *within* the older generation (for example, being not just old, but old and much more – a woman, a man, a disabled woman or man, or whatever else contributes to a person's unique make-up). What makes people different can also provide grounds in some people's minds for treating them unfairly, and so many older people not only have to contend with ageism, but also discrimination because of their ethnicity, disability, gender, and other forms of discrimination that can blight their lives.

In effect, older people can suffer a double whammy – they continue to have their lives adversely affected by a combination of forms of discrimination but, because one of the effects of ageism is to make any aspects of identity other than age 'invisible', these experiences go largely un- or under-recognised and un- or under-addressed.

From Where I'm Sitting: Marcus's Story

Who'd have thought I'd have cried so much when Her Majesty died? I don't mean the queen, I'm talking about my pigeon. I was very fond of that pigeon but still, she was only a bird and I wasn't expecting to find myself so upset over her. Yesterday, when the nurse called round to change the dressing on my leg, I started getting upset again and when I told him why, I thought he'd think I was being silly. But he didn't. In fact, he said how sorry he was for my loss. 'Marcus', he said, 'that must be really hard for you because I know that she was the last one and that you're going to miss having racing pigeons in your life'.

I know he's busy, but it really helped when he sat with me for a while and said he wasn't surprised at how upset I'd got because he could see that it wasn't just about the pigeon, but about one thing after another going wrong with my health, and my world shrinking the more difficult I find it to get out and about, especially now that my eyes are getting affected too.

Having those lads come round and move the pigeon loft to where I could see it helped a lot, and one of them had been looking after this one, with me telling him what to do, but there'll be no more now. He's right. Now that I think about it, I feel like I've been knocked down every time I've tried to get up again lately. First there was having to move out here where I didn't know anyone, but that was better than the racist aggravation I'd been getting for years on that other estate. I'll never leave that behind though because I carry the taunts in my head. I don't think anyone round here knows about what I've had to go through.

They just think I'm a sad old bloke who doesn't like going out much, but they don't know me at all if that's the case. I'd love to get out and about, especially in the countryside around here, but my legs won't carry me now. I used to walk for miles and miles surveying hedgerows and pathways. That's another part of me gone and I don't suppose I'll get it back. Eyes gone, legs gone, pigeons gone, and sometimes when I see racist attacks on the news, my faith in humanity too. I used to get angry, but now I just get sad.

Having to accept that, while life can continue to be exhilarating and fun, losses are likely to feature significantly and often

We spent Chapter 7 considering that, in old age, not only are death-related losses likely to feature in people's lives, but also other forms of loss are too, though the significance of these is often not appreciated. It is this lack of understanding that can make grieving those losses doubly difficult because, where something isn't recognised as being a problem, then potentially helpful resources will not be offered to those who would stand to benefit. Any of us who have experienced the loss of someone or something that was important to us will know how difficult that can be. But, if we have had people comforting us, validating that we are going through something difficult, and offering us strategies for coping, then we can confirm that these things can be a great help. Their understanding can't take the pain of loss away, but it can often help to make the grieving process a little less painful. Imagine, then, how it might feel if that validation and support aren't there because it is assumed that they aren't needed. So, once again, a double whammy: more loss experiences and less help with grieving them.

The point has already been made that the problems old age brings along with it don't line up in an orderly fashion waiting to be addressed, but more often feed into one another, sometimes making things better and sometimes worse. As far as losses are concerned, grieving can be tiring, debilitating and sometimes devastating, which can result in a loss of enthusiasm and energy at the very point where coping reserves need to be drawn on. And, as you'll probably have experienced yourself, when reserves are low, everything feels more of a challenge. For example, coping with being discriminated against is likely to be very difficult to deal with but, even more so when one's coping resources are depleted, and then depleted even more, by the frequency of losses experienced.

Later we will look at the overcoming of challenges and will focus on resilience in the face of the hard knocks that can be a feature of old age. As part of this we'll look in particular at the existence, or otherwise, of networks of support when older people are negotiating difficult times.

Having to face up to their mortality

This is not to suggest that older people spend their days constantly worrying about dying. Far from it as, for many, their old age is a time when they enjoy and celebrate life, and the fact that they will have fewer tomorrows than yesterdays may be one of the reasons why they throw themselves into making the best of the time they expect to have left.

Nevertheless, life is, of course, finite and coping with that is something that some people find more difficult than others because it brings into sharp focus such questions as: What have I done with my life? Do I have any regrets? Will I have time to make sure that I don't? Will I have to live longer than I would like to? and so on. For example, I have known some older people to say that they are worried that, when they die, no-one will remember them. This is not necessarily about low self-esteem, but because they consider themselves to have lived an 'ordinary life' and so will not leave an enduring legacy that is marked in some way. Reviewing one's life, exploring spiritual matters, is often done in private, and so it may be that someone you support is experiencing problems without anyone else being aware. And, because of that, they may be losing out on the support that having their concerns validated as important can bring, and the knowledge that others grapple with those things too, can also bring.

And then there's the 'bits falling off'

What we have thought about above are just a few of the many challenges that can add to those that are caused by the inevitability (unless you are a superhero of some sort) of some degree of physical decline in old age. As we have already discussed, old age does not necessarily equate with illness and disability but, however much care we take of ourselves, our physical bodies eventually wear out. For example, our hearing, eyesight, and joints become less efficient. And that's if we start from a baseline of being relatively healthy: many people age with existing disabilities, chronic conditions such as asthma or diabetes, and possibly mental health problems too, like anxiety or depression.

Accepting the inevitability of physical decline is one thing, but consider how much more difficult that becomes when you have to worry about whether the associated health challenges it brings will be taken seriously, as in comments reflected by many older people I have encountered who, on visiting healthcare practitioners, have received comments such as 'what do you expect at your age?'

The same level of support and intervention as anyone else would have been my answer!

Facing challenges independently of each other and, in combination, can make each challenge more difficult to cope with. But coping with challenges is what people do, otherwise we wouldn't have any older people left to support! We'll aim in Chapter 12, the final one, to end on a positive note by turning our attention to the *overcoming* of challenges, and how we can help with that. Before we do so, however, we'll pay some attention, in Chapter 11, to the challenges and opportunities that living in 'The Digital Age' presents for some older people.

Exercise 10

For the purpose of this exercise, either focus on one of the older people you support, or have supported, or try to imagine your future self. Ask yourself the following questions:

In what ways do you think that gender makes a difference, or has the potential to, in respect of the challenges people face in old age?

In what ways do you think that being rich or poor makes a difference in respect of the challenges people face in old age?

In what ways do you think that being a member of an ethnic minority or majority makes a difference, or has the potential to, in respect of the challenges people face in old age?

Over to you ...

What steps can you take to help you always to remember that the older people you support are possibly facing many different challenges?

CHAPTER 11

The older people you support are living in the same digital age as you are

We are currently living in an era which has come to be known as 'the digital age' and have experienced unprecedentedly rapid technological change over the past several decades. What characterises the digital age is the widespread use of digital technologies that have a very significant impact on how we work, communicate and spend our leisure time – pretty well every aspect of our lives. Some people find the potential that it offers exciting, some find it daunting, but for most it's a mixture of both. In this chapter we'll look at how it affects the lives of older people and, given that we're focusing on the ways in which you can support them, the particular implications for older people who have come to rely on others for the help they need to be able to live, as far as possible, life as they want to live it.

We'll consider the potential for technological advances in the digital world to enrich older people's enjoyment of life by contributing to their wellbeing, but it is important to remember that not all older people have access to digital technology, and even for those who do, these changes can be daunting and confusing, and can leave them open to abuse. It is also important to remember that, like any other sector of the population, there will be a great deal of diversity in terms of experience, technical competence, personal preference, opportunity and so on, when it comes to reaping the benefits and avoiding the disadvantages that being party to this way of communicating and managing our day to day living entails. As we have already explored, ageism contributes to the construction and maintenance of the stereotype of older people as necessarily uninformed and wary of technological change, but we only have to look at the huge number of older people who engage with the digital world competently and optimistically to see that this is not necessarily the case.

DOI: 10.4324/9781041054481-12

Before looking at some of the potential consequences of digital inclusion (or exclusion) for the older people you support, and the role you can play in helping them to benefit from it, but also be safeguarded from its potential dangers, let's take a brief look at the matter of access to the technology.

Is digital connectivity open to all?

It is clear that older people in general are increasingly using digital technology (for example, having smart phones, using Internet banking and so on) but it is difficult to know whether this reflects a rise in what is called 'digital literacy' (the understanding and skills necessary for someone to engage with the technology) or not, because it might be the case that other people are helping them or doing the transactions or searches on their behalf. Exclusion from digital connectivity might in part, therefore, be accounted for by people having access to the technology but lacking the understanding necessary to take advantage of it. This might be the case if the person in question has a cognitive impairment of some sort – dementia or brain damage perhaps.

However, we also need to consider that some of the older people you support may be excluded from accessing the many opportunities that being digitally connected can offer because of the relationship between economic disadvantage and the 'digital divide' – a term used to describe the gap between those who have access to information technologies and those who don't. Getting, and staying, digitally connected can be an expensive undertaking and, if we take into account that many older people are economically disadvantaged (over 2 million and rising, according to the charity Age UK) one which may not be considered a priority when money is tight. That some older people are *not* digitally excluded suggests that economic status *is* part of the dynamic and that age is not the only factor to consider.

Another issue to consider is whether reliable broadband is available, as being without that (as is often the case in rural areas) can be problematic for older people who may already be disadvantaged by living in isolated areas where opportunities to remain connected to the rest of their communities, and the world outside their homes, can be hard to find. It is true that wi-fi access may be available in libraries, cafes and other meeting places but if mobility is impaired, a car is not available, and public transport is less than optimal, accessing such opportunities may not be easy for some. It seems fair to say, then, that digital connectivity is not open to all in equal measure, and some older people will lose out on the opportunities it offers unless this disparity is addressed.

Opportunities and threats

We'll look below at four aspects in which we can argue that digital technology has the potential to enrich or safeguard the lives of older people, while also recognising that (i) barriers to realising that potential exist and (ii) outcomes might not be in the interests of the people you support.

Accessing healthcare

It seems fair to say that healthcare in the UK has been revolutionised in recent decades, with the digitisation of patient records and appointment booking systems for example, and the use of Artificial Intelligence technology to contribute to research into, diagnosis of, and treatments for a wide range of health conditions. Not everyone is aware of the extent to which digital technologies are routinely being used in healthcare and delving into this field can be fascinating and enlightening to say the least. You'll no doubt be aware of some of the consequences of digitisation if your work schedules and so on are managed online and GPS technology is used to streamline allocation of visits, and for monitoring of your adherence to timetables and schedules, which is increasingly likely to be the case.

Where it might become more obvious to the people you support is where increased use of digital technology intersects with their daily lives and needs. Increasingly, for example, the ordering of prescriptions and booking of GP or community nurse appointments needs to be done online. This no doubt works to the benefit of the healthcare providers but not always to the users of those services, especially if they don't have the skills necessary to negotiate the often complex processes. It is possible to see a power imbalance in situations such as when older patients are seen at hospital appointments and so on and told about things they need to do (procedures and medication protocols to follow, and sometimes self-monitoring of conditions, for example). But while these protocols and instructions will be well-understood by the clinicians imparting that information (because it is something they are doing very regularly) those on the receiving end will probably be hearing about this for the first time and might struggle to take in and retain that new information in what is often a pressurised situation, or at least one that feels pressurised, especially if they are being asked to engage with technology that is new to them.

Living in the digital age benefits many older people's health and wellbeing in a multitude of ways, directly and indirectly – too many to cover in a short section such as this – and so I would urge you to explore these issues in more detail when you can make time to do so. You might already have had cause to think about the benefits and disadvantages to the older people you support of digital technology by being able to see for yourself the difference particular initiatives make to them. For example, they might benefit from online consultations in their own homes and a whole range of assistive technologies, such as monitoring systems which can detect when a person may have fallen, or be unwell, because of changes in their usual routines (for example, a reduction or absence of trips to the toilet or kitchen, or a change in body temperature). Or you might be able to detect a change in their mood after being enabled to engage with loved ones online.

On a more negative note, have you found yourself wondering why, if the technology to enrich older people's health and wellbeing exists, it is not made available to all and whether living in the digital age involves dealing with threats, as well as taking up opportunities? Does the potential exist for the voice of older people to be lost or undermined unless they have the initiative, skills and opportunity to engage with healthcare providers on an equal footing?

Complex issues, undoubtedly, but plenty of food for thought.

Managing household affairs

If you're one of those people who use their smartphone, or other digital device, to manage your life with an app for everything from bill paying to recipe finding, you might wonder how people ever managed to run their household affairs before such technology became available. But manage people certainly did – in different but no less competent ways. As with the negotiating of healthcare systems, some older people quickly adapt to the expectation that transactions such as shopping, paying fuel bills and so on will be made online. And some would say that this makes their lives easier, especially if getting out and about has become difficult for them, although there is a downside to that, given that it has the potential to reduce the number and quality of interpersonal encounters that many isolated older people crave. However, for those who aren't digitally connected, or lack the skills, initiative or confidence to make use of the opportunities it offers, this trend towards dealing with everything online has the potential to make managing household affairs more, rather than less, difficult. And, furthermore, it can contribute to a situation where some older people feel like matters are out of their control because they can't easily see where their money is coming from or going out to. This information is, of course, usually available if you know where to look for it, but therein lies the problem, as knowing where to look is an acquired skill and systems are not always user-friendly. In such situations, financial abuse is not always easy for a victim to spot, which is particularly worrying given that older people are often targeted by criminals looking to trick them into parting with their cash or security information.

Over time, as more and more people age with the skills needed to survive and thrive in the digital age, managing one's domestic affairs in this way is likely to become second nature, although it remains the case that those who cannot access the technology for economic reasons, or because of cognitive problems, will probably still be disadvantaged. Currently, though, within this present cohort of older people that you support, there are likely to be many who find the rapid rate of technological change, and the implications it has for how they live (or are expected to live) their lives unsettling, disempowering and even frightening.

In your work as a carer, have you witnessed situations where some of the older people you support seem to be overwhelmed by new technologies and the expectation that they engage with them? Or, conversely, where they are able to engage with it and enjoy doing so? Are you aware of any initiatives that could help those without the skills to be able to acquire them, or have ongoing support to use them to their advantage? Have you seen, or can you envisage, older care recipients who themselves have the skills needed to survive and thrive in the digital age providing that learning and support to those older people who don't?

Being socially connected

While some people are happy with their own company, many of those who cannot leave their homes easily in order to meet friends for a chat, or to go to a church meeting or another social function *do* miss the companionship and stimulation that such activities offer – especially if they have always been gregarious and found pleasure in engaging with the outside world before circumstances conspired to make it seem that their world is closing in on them. In relation to self-esteem, back in 1996 Crossley was making the point that we need interaction with other people – he used the term 'intersubjectivity' – to help us make sense of our place in the world. Part of that understanding of our place in the world is to have it reflected back to us that we are valued human beings, so what Crossley was writing about then is still very relevant now in situations where intersubjectivity is not easy to achieve if a dependent and isolated older person isn't able to get that validation in the 'real' world, and their self-esteem suffers as a consequence. Could being socially connected via a 'virtual world' help? The answer is probably yes, given that there are now lots of online platforms which provide an opportunity to engage with other people (as long as they are digitally connected) in real time. Some older people find this enough to counteract the sense of isolation and disconnection from the world, but I have personally encountered people for whom engaging with others in this way has only served to highlight what they perceive to be a decline in their ability to get out and about like they used to. In such situations, do you think that this outlook could be 'reframed' as that living in the digital age is something that gives them an opportunity to use their personality, life experience and social skills to support others in ways that don't need to draw on what it is that they can no longer do? That is, a way for them to boost their self-esteem by focusing on what they *can* do, rather on what they *can't* do?

As well as facilitating engagement with other people for its own sake – just for the enjoyment of communicating with other people rather than talking to oneself – modern digital technologies can help like-minded older people to get together as interest-based groups to discuss shared hopes, dreams, worries and so on and, if the interest is there, to take action to address issues that have been raised within those groups. And, talking of like-minded people with shared interests, it is no longer necessary for people to meet face to face to have a game of chess, cards, bingo, bridge, or Mah-Jong, for example. While some might miss the social aspect of sitting around a table in the 'real' world, digital technology offers the potential for a different type of social community to develop to fill that void.

Do any of the people you support use voice-activated assistants (such as Alexa or Siri) to help them manage their daily affairs, such as providing reminders, accessing information, and so on? If so, do you think that such technology might also be providing another function – that is, to provide companionship and the comfort of hearing another voice in an otherwise empty house or flat?

Expanding, rather than diminishing, horizons

As we have discussed in earlier chapters, the older people you support are still on a journey through life and, although ageist stereotyping would have us believe otherwise, still capable (even if their cognitive faculties are not what they once were) of ongoing learning and personal development. And, indeed, many older people actively seek opportunities to keep on learning about themselves, the world around them and developments in the sectors they once worked in or had an interest or expertise in – agriculture, medicine, botany, climatology, travel – the list is endless. There is a growing trend for full- and part-time educational courses that were traditionally offered by learning providers such as universities and colleges, and which required learners to travel to those places in order to participate, to now be offered as online courses, in many cases the online option being the only option. It is not hard to see that this way of accessing formal educational opportunities could be beneficial for those older people who cannot leave their homes, or cannot do so easily or safely. However, as we have already noted, accessing such opportunities relies on being digitally connected and not every older person is connected, can afford to pay the fees charged or has the skills or confidence to participate.

Of course, ongoing learning does not have to be through formal learning. We can learn informally by reading, watching TV or listening to the radio, and indeed just from our life experience and from other people's insights and opinions. Though it brings with it issues around the trustworthiness of what we come across on the Internet – fake news, digitally altered images and other potential distortions – it would seem that having access to 'the information highway' could be considered a potential benefit to older people who remain curious and concerned about the world they live in, while facing restrictions on being a part of it. And more than that, it has the potential to enable them to contribute to the processes of knowledge exchange through discussion forums and the like, and to have the voice that living in an ageist society often denies them.

One fairly recent technological advance that has huge potential for enabling learning and development is that of Virtual Reality (VR). This technology enables computer-generated, immersive environments to be created so that, if wearing a VR headset, one can experience and participate in scenarios that feel real but are not. VR technology is sometimes used as a distraction technique to take someone's mind off what could otherwise be experienced as a scary or painful medical procedure and in the gaming world to create such environments as fantasy worldscapes. In terms of the people you support, are you aware of, or can you imagine, how VR technology could support ongoing learning or enhance quality of life? Two applications come to my mind:

1. creating a virtual environment in which people can be seen to be participating in a group exercise class for their general health or for rehabilitation after

surgery or an illness, and in which they are able to 'participate' by making their bodies move in the real world but be reflected in the virtual one, and

2. being 'transported' to a representation of a place that holds significance for them in the real world (for example a seaside location, a forest, a mountain climb or the village they grew up in), so that they can 'visit' those places or engage with those experiences, without even having to leave their chair. As you can no doubt appreciate, this has the potential to enrich quality of life in many ways but particularly in relation to stimulating memory and in the management of anxiety.

As mentioned earlier, dependent older people can experience life as a narrowing of their horizons but perhaps you will be able to appreciate that VR technology offers the possibility of widening horizons and welcome that its use may become more widespread?

TIP! Consider whether those people you support have the same awareness as you might have of the opportunities that digital technologies offer, or the opportunity or desire to engage with those opportunities.

From Where I'm Sitting: Big Joe and Little Joe's Story

Big Joe is my grandfather and, as we live in the same house and my father is also called Joe and he does too (we just call him Joe) things can get a bit confusing at times, as you can imagine. So, everyone in the family and our local community uses those names to differentiate us from each other. Although I'm called Little Joe, I'm over 6 feet tall and I tower above Big Joe, especially as he's got osteoporosis now and walks with a stoop. Dad and I both love him, and it's a pleasure having him live with us. We don't need an encyclopedia because there doesn't seem to be anything he doesn't know about and he loves reading books and watching documentaries on the TV. Me and Big Joe used to spend hours together in the evenings but lately that doesn't tend to happen because he likes his TV and I tend to go for what I think is a quicker and easier way to get information and pleasure – my phone. Makes sense to me but not, apparently, to him.

Or that's how it used to be before he discovered the Internet. He used to say that it was just a fad and 'no good will come of it' but he's a convert now. The other day I mentioned that I was trying to find time to go to the travel agent in town to look at holiday possibilities and he said why bother? I thought he meant that he didn't feel up to going anywhere but it turns out he'd looked at various options online and was about to talk to us about them. And when his carer arrived this morning to help him have a bath he asked him whether he'd like to go scuba diving with him, via his 'wonderful new friend' the Internet, of course. And he did! Better get downstairs pronto. Big Joe has arranged for the three of us to do a tour of The Taj Mahal. He's fulfilling his dreams now in a way he never thought possible. Doesn't call it a fad now!

It is beyond your duty as a carer to ensure that all of the older people you support are digitally connected and engaged but what you can play a part in is, where someone is not engaging in the digital word and the positive opportunities it offers, or are confused or frightened by it, you could point them in the direction of people (fellow care recipients, perhaps?) or organisations that can help. Some people might actively choose not to engage with the digital age, preferring to live their lives according to long-practiced routines that might seem cumbersome and time-consuming to people who have become used to using apps on their phones to pay bills and so on, but which continue to give those older people a sense of security through familiarity, and a sense of control and autonomy which comes from 'doing things my own way'. And that's fine because choice is one of the values that I would hope informs your practice, but where the lack of engagement is due to lack of opportunity or skills, then you will be well-placed to notice where people may be experiencing a sense of disadvantage, and to deliver that message (or help older people to do so themselves) to those who have more power than you do to make change happen. In doing so, you can make a positive difference, which I'm sure you'll agree is all part of being the best practitioner you can be.

Exercise 11

If you support just one older person, and they're willing to help, ask them the following questions. If you support more than one, it might be interesting and informative to invite them to do a small survey. Remember to let them know that this is an informal exercise and the results will not be shared with anyone without their permission. Unless the person has a severe degree of cognitive impairment, most will be able to provide some response but may need prompts to aid with their recall.

1. How did they pay their utility bills 30 years ago? How do they pay them now? Which do they prefer and why?
2. How did they shop 30 years ago? How do they shop now? Which do they prefer and why?

3. How did they choose a holiday 30 years ago? How do they choose a holiday now? Which do they prefer and why?
4. How did they communicate with their family and friends 30 years ago? How do they do so now? Which do they prefer and why?
5. How did they get access to a GP or community nurse 30 years ago? How do they get access to a GP or community nurse now? Which system do they prefer and why?

Has this exercise produced any results that have given you food for thought about the benefits and disadvantages of digital inclusivity in eldercare?

Over to you ...
What steps can you take to always ensure that the older people you support are getting the best out of living in the digital age?

CHAPTER 12

The older people you support are able to draw on a range of strengths and resilience factors

While there's no doubting that old age brings challenges along with it, and we need to appreciate how difficult it can be to face any or all of them, there is no doubting too that people tend to find ways to overcome them, or at least make the best of things. If it were the case that older people lost their resilience along with other losses they experience then we wouldn't have the resourceful and spirited people in our lives that we do and people wouldn't have the positive and affirming old age that many, and possibly the majority, enjoy. So what is resilience, how do older people become and remain resilient, and how can we help to promote it in situations where life proves particularly challenging for those we support?

What is resilience?

Resilience can be described as the process, or set of processes, whereby people are able to bounce back from adversity – from something that they have found challenging – so that they can get back to how they felt and were able to function before experiencing 'being knocked back'. Resilience isn't something we all have in equal measure. Nor is it purely the case that some individuals are more resilient than others (Tanner, 2020). For instance, if we take the example of being made redundant, we can see that not everyone will respond to what might, on the face of it, seem like a catastrophic and life-changing challenge in the same way. One person might, once they have got over the initial shock, start thinking about how they are going to deal with the situation. That is, their resilience is such that they have the emotional energy to 'pick themselves up, dust themselves down, and start all over again'. Another person who, for whatever reason, is not so

DOI: 10.4324/9781041054481-13

resilient might find that they just cannot manage to do that – what has happened is something they are not able to recover from.

We should not put this down purely to individual characteristics, however, as there are a number of other factors which can help account for why some people are more resilient than others. These include:

- The nature of previous episodes of adversity;
- The frequency of previous episodes of adversity;
- The duration of previous episodes of adversity;
- The interrelationships across different forms of adversity being experienced at the same time;
- What they may have been able to learn from previous experience; and
- The level and quality of support people have in their lives.

It is fair to say that some people, or groups of people, are more likely to face more challenges in life than others – those experiencing poverty, discrimination in one or more forms, and poor health, to name just a few. We have to consider that everyone has a limit to what we can cope with before being overwhelmed and this will be affected by circumstances. It isn't simply a case of whether we are weak or strong. Resilience isn't something we are born with, it is something we can develop, so how is it that some people find enough resilience to overcome the adversity they experience, rather than lie down and take it?

How do people become resilient?

Some people get a good grounding in terms of resilience by being brought up within families where there is a good role model for demonstrating that difficulties can be overcome. For example, there may have been someone to whom others tended to turn for help when things were tough – the one who always seemed to find a silver lining in any cloud. Resilience can also be enhanced by experience and people in their old age will have had decades of practice in facing life challenges. Those in their old age now will have faced any number of issues that have given them concern – family change or even tragedy, political upheavals that have resulted in policy changes that may not have worked to their advantage, disruptive or debilitating illness or accidents to themselves or family and friends and a variety of losses as we have already touched on. But they will also have had decades of experience in developing strategies for how to deal with those issues and, if they have been able to come out the other side of them and back to 'normal' relatively unscathed, then they will have had decades of learning from what worked and what didn't. Having a lengthy period available for review can also help build resilience, in the sense that it can sometimes help to keep things in perspective (as in the way some people approach challenges with a 'been here before' approach).

While some people seem to be more resilient than others, it would be a mistake to assume that whether a person is resilient and copes well with adversity, or isn't and doesn't, can be put down to individual characteristics or skills and that only. For example, there are other factors that can have an effect on resilience because they make challenges easier to overcome for some people than for others. These include:

Affluence

Not every problem can be overcome by throwing money at it, of course, but financial security – and insecurity – can be a factor when people are facing difficulties and trying to overcome them. This is because some of the challenges arise from living life in poverty, and some of the solutions to those challenges are beyond the reach of those living in poverty (and many older people are, especially if they are living on meagre state pensions because their circumstances earlier in life have not enabled them to build up savings or put money into the private pension schemes that can help fund a comfortable lifestyle in their old age). For example, consider how some older people have access to private healthcare, and others do not, and the implications that having to wait a long time for debilitating conditions such as arthritis to be treated can have for a person's capacity to remain resilient in the face of this and other challenges.

Social support

While resilience can be fostered by having high levels of financial capital, it can also be fostered by having high levels of what is referred to as *social* capital. This refers to the extent and quality of the network of people and organisations on which people can draw for support during times of adversity (and, conversely, to which they can contribute so that they are there to provide support to others when they are, or have been, in a position to). This network can include family; friends; reliable people they have come into contact with through going to work, church, or social activities; contacts they have made through the helping professions; and so on. Contacts in influential positions can raise someone's social capital 'bank balance' quite considerably because they have the potential to be able to use their power to influence others to act in someone's interest when this might not otherwise have been the case because of competing interests. The support of others, therefore, can be a major factor in promoting resilience but, as we see below, for those in old age, this potential is not always realised.

Social validation

By this I mean the existence, or otherwise, of a mindset that doesn't accept ageism, and of a strong commitment to challenging the powerful and hard-to-shift ageist assumption that older people are all frail, powerless and defeatist, rather than members of a sector of society which contains as many competent and resilient individuals as any other. Some older people find it easier than others to ignore the ageist messages that they are likely to hear on a regular basis – about being a drain on resources, past their sell-by date, an old fogey and so on – and, indeed, some make a concerted effort to prove the ageist assumptions and expectations wrong. But, especially if you've had to face the many and profound challenges that accompany old age, it can be difficult to hold on to a positive sense of self and to feel that you are a valued member of the community and society in which you live. And that's probably not good news in respect of maintaining resilience. Being aware of, or better still being part of, initiatives that challenge the negative stereotyping of old age sounds like better news. I'm thinking here of initiatives, such as intergenerational ones, where older and younger generations come together to swap skills and perspectives to their mutual benefit, and the University of the Third Age, where retired people engage in the learning and development that ageist stereotyping suggests is not something that should be aspired to in old age.

Take some time out here to think about other initiatives that you are aware of which have the potential to help the older people you support know that they are still valued. If we think of life as a series of challenges, then we should respect older people for their survival skills and call on their expertise to show us how it's done.

What can adversely affect that resilience?

We have had a brief look at what can promote resilience, so now let's look at the other side of the coin: what can get in the way. We've already looked at how loss, after loss, after loss can adversely affect resilience, so let's look here at some other potential obstacles to give you food for thought. Feel free to add to the list if you can come up with more.

Profound and multiple experiences of discrimination

We have already discussed how discrimination on the grounds of ethnicity, gender, sexuality, class, disability, and other bases for treating some people less favourably than others does not stop once someone comes to be defined as old, although ageist thinking would have us believe that nothing else is of significance at that point. You will no doubt have worked with, or met, enough older people to put that particular myth to bed because you will have seen the ongoing discrimination in action in their lives – older people from ethnic minorities who don't have their preferred language or lifestyle preferences respected when support is provided, for example. If you're feeling emotionally strong and confident that you have a right to insist on being respected for the unique individual that you are, then this might feel achievable but, if you are led to believe that you and your individuality don't matter, then finding your voice is not likely to be easy.

Low social capital

Building up at least some degree of a network of support is something that is likely to have been possible over a lifetime, but *maintaining* that network can become problematic for a number of reasons. These include:

- the loss of relatives and friends of a similar age who may have died, moved away, or are unable to help because of their own incapacities;
- the loss of community networks of support when someone has to, or chooses to, move to live nearer to their families, or to live communally in assisted living facilities or residential homes;
- becoming housebound and therefore unable to attend clubs and societies to which they have been able to contribute and where membership will have had the potential to make them aware that other people are interested in their welfare; and
- even when not housebound, it can be difficult to maintain social networks if you are unable to drive, and public transport is inaccessible or non-existent.

Impaired understanding

It is possible that some of those older people that you support need that help because of conditions that affect their understanding or memory. Some people might not have a full awareness of the difficulties they face but where a person does, but struggles to find ways to cope with them, this can add an extra layer of difficulty where being able to 'bounce back from adversity' is concerned.

Being affected by depression

It can be the case that an older person understands the challenges but, if they are depressed, feel overwhelmed by them, and lack the emotional energy to fuel their capacity to 'bounce back'. And where this is the case, the lack of emotional energy can feed into their spiritual wellbeing, in the sense that it can contribute to feelings of poor self-worth in general and the internalisation of ageist assumptions of inferiority to which we referred in Chapter 6.

A lack of focus on strengths

As with all people, of all ages, older people have strengths as well as weaknesses. As we have seen, though, strengths can be overlooked or minimised when weaknesses become more apparent, such as when they become significantly reliant on other people for support to live their lives. There has been a history, in social care, of support staff drawing on a strengths perspective when supporting people to overcome the challenges they face in life – that is, helping them to recognise what their strengths are and how they can use them to best effect in the circumstances they find themselves in (Thompson and Cox, 2020).

However, the potential for a strengths perspective to promote 'bouncebackability' in the older population doesn't seem to have been drawn on to quite the same extent as with other vulnerable and oppressed groups in society. Tanner (2020) suggests that older people living with chronic health conditions may perceive resilience as just being able to keep going, rather than having aspirations to 'bounce back' to a former state of independence, and we need to take their perceptions on board. But maybe you'd agree with me that it is not in the interests of dependent older people to disregard or underuse a strengths approach in eldercare given the many, many strengths that exist within that group of people. You might want to look at the care assessment and planning documents that the people you support will probably have copies of, even if you don't. You are likely to see 'weaknesses' or 'needs' being recorded, but do you see any evidence of 'strengths' being mentioned specifically? If the answer is yes, then that's great but if it is no, why do you think that might be?

From Where I'm Sitting: Rita's Story

My daughter had been on at me to buck up for a long time. I know what she meant, I must come across as a right moaner. 'Mum', she used to say, 'where's your sparkle gone?' And I used to say, 'I don't know, Priya, but I wish it would come back'. I'd been feeling down for ages and was beginning to think it was depression. I was watching some people my age on the TV talking about how they were getting busier the older they got and it got me thinking that maybe that's what had been getting me down — I'm not doing anything of any importance. I couldn't see myself doing anything like that — volunteering like they were. When I thought about what I could do in the way of helping out anywhere I couldn't think of a single thing I would be able to offer, especially since these kidney problems tie me down these days.

One day, when Priya came round and found me crying she got me to admit what it was all about. 'I just feel so useless', I said. But Priya wasn't having any of that. She sat down with me and started a list of the positive differences I make in people's lives. She started with the time I spend helping her children with their reading and sums and me being the person who helps her with her bookkeeping and tax stuff.

Before long we'd got quite a long list, which surprised me and did wonders for my self-esteem. I started off thinking I was a useless old lady, but now I know that the family, and a lot of my friends too, would be stuck without me. Funny how they'd all been thinking of me as 'the go-to person' when I myself was thinking that I hadn't got anything to offer. I've kept that list and I add to it whenever it occurs to me that I'm being 'useful'. I'll have to get a bigger piece of paper soon!

How can we help?

Let's start with the strengths perspective that we've just been focusing on. You may well already be promoting this perspective in your own practice, by helping people to be as independent as possible by reminding them of their strengths and helping them to find ways to continue using and building on them, while also helping them with their areas of difficulty (those things they can no longer do). By doing so, you are helping people to continue on their life journey in difficult circumstances, rather than helping them to accept that their life is over or has to be lived on someone else's terms. If you aren't promoting that in your practice, then ask yourself what it is that you *are* doing, and whether your approach is likely to help them to deal with problems when they arise. You might find the next few suggestions useful if you are committed to helping the people you support to recognise, and be able to draw on, the range of strengths and resilience factors that can help them to stay positive in the face of difficulties faced.

1. Paying attention to the language we use. Language is a very powerful transmitter of ideas, underlying assumptions and so on. For example, if we refer to older people as 'the elderly', it conveys an understanding of them as a sector of society without recognition that we are talking here about *individuals* and *people*. Using the term 'older people' or 'elders' instead conveys an appreciation of that. Language choice can also be a powerful ally in terms of promoting resilience because it can help to challenge the association in people's minds between old age and frailty. So, we can help by, wherever possible, using language that promotes the reality that there are a lot of positives in old age, and challenges the assumption that it is always and inevitably a negative phase of life. We will not be able to change things on our own but, if we are sensitive to how the language we use can make things better or worse, then we can certainly play a part in making old age as much about the overcoming of problems as it is about experiencing them.

2. Encouraging people to think about the life they would like to be living. It would seem to make sense that if people are happy with their lives, then they are likely to be more resilient in the face of hard knocks than they would be if their 'normal' is an unhappy or unfulfilled life. Looking out for ways in which the people you support can help others (the reciprocity we talked about in Chapter 6) can help to counteract any feelings of 'uselessness' they might be feeling as a result of having to rely heavily on others. So maybe you could have a conversation with them about reciprocity?

3. Having as one of your guiding principles that your role is to help the people you support to keep on living until they die – that is, to pursue whatever life goals they still want to pursue until they draw their last breath. It is likely that they will be vulnerable in some way, and so, as part of your duties, you will be involved in helping to protect them from harm. However, if that becomes the *only* consideration, then ask yourself whether this might get in the way of their wellbeing in other ways. Hopes and aspirations for the future are something we all have, but these can be overlooked if care is planned and delivered with a mindset that doesn't see older people as having much of a future to worry about. Decisions about care planning are unlikely to be your call alone to make, but one thing you can do is to get such concerns as you might have on the agenda for discussion with managers and colleagues.

4. Helping older people to develop new supportive networks where existing ones have become difficult to maintain. This is likely to require creative

thinking but, where there's a will there's usually a way. For example, developments in communications technology allow for 'virtual' supportive networks to be created and maintained even when someone isn't able to leave their house (or even their bed).

Throughout this manual we have noted that older people in need of support from others often have a fight on their hands to maintain a positive sense of identity in the face of negativity about their abilities and worth. I hope that what we have discussed in this final chapter has reminded you of the important role you can play in helping those you support to maintain their 'bouncebackability' or reclaim it where they have lost it.

Exercise 12

What are your coping strategies for the times when things aren't going so well for you? What inner strengths and outside help can you call on to help you overcome difficulties you might be facing?

Are you able to identify the coping strategies that the people you support use to help them cope with the difficulties *they* face?

Do you think there is scope for learning from each other?

How might you be able to help the people you support to feel positive about their strengths when the focus is so often on their weaknesses?

Over to you ...

What steps can you take to help you always to remember that the older people you support are able to draw on a range of strengths and resilience factors?

Conclusion

In the previous chapters we have explored some of the reasons why negative, demeaning and disempowering assumptions about old age in general and dependent older people in particular continue to be influential. But we have also explored how, if our practice is underpinned by anti-ageist values (those things that we think are important) then we can play a significant part in undermining those assumptions in the interests of promoting a good quality of life for those people in our care. So, to recap, we began by looking at ageism – what it is and what it does – before moving on to explore some of the consequences for how older people who need our support are perceived and how we can challenge those perceptions by working in ways which reflect the dignity and respect that those older people we work with are owed in a just society. We discussed how they:

- Are unique and multidimensional and so it is unfair to treat them as if they are all the same. Take a moment to think about how that would feel if it happened to you;
- Have life left to live, however old they are. That is, they have a future dimension to their lives;
- Are as entitled as anyone else to palliative care should they need it. Old age on its own is not a justification for denying them what they and their loved ones would consider as 'good' a death as possible;
- Are not problems just by their very definition as old and dependent and that there are other perspectives on 'the problem' of old age;
- Can, and want to, engage in reciprocity. That is, they have much to give back to society but are often conceptualised as being a burden rather than an asset;

DOI: 10.4324/9781041054481-14

- Are as affected by loss as anyone else and may feel cumulative losses more, rather than less, deeply;
- Are entitled to take risks, even though we and their loved ones might not consider such behaviour to be in their best interests;
- Are entitled to have their own expertise recognised when decision-making about their care arrangements takes place. That is, the power imbalance between older service users and 'expert professionals' needs to be addressed;
- Are currently living in a digital era which is characterised by rapid change which both poses threats and offers opportunities if they can access the technologies; and
- Face many and varied challenges but have strengths and resilience to draw on in meeting them.

As I mentioned in the Introduction, covering every aspect of working with older people in need of support has always been beyond the scope of this manual, and indeed any other, because eldercare is a complex and changing phenomenon and nobody should claim to have 'all the right answers'. It is asking too much of yourself to aspire to getting things right every time and you shouldn't berate yourself for not always being aware that your practice could be said to contravene a principle of anti-ageist practice. What is important is that you recognise when this is happening and embark on a learning journey that helps you to develop awareness of *your* part in the dynamic relationship between the person who needs support and the person who supplies it and strive to reach as near as is possible to the absolute ideal of anti-ageist practice. Reaching that absolute ideal is, arguably, beyond what anyone involved in eldercare can expect to achieve but it is in our striving to do so that we can play a significant role in challenging the myth that old age is necessarily a time of decline rather than growth, and that older people are by definition incompetent.

If you're reading this after a quick skim read of the manual, then I hope you will have been inspired to revisit it with the intention of engaging with the exercises, and recording your own thoughts on how what you read relates to your own particular circumstances. If you have reached this point having already done that, then congratulations on having built on the manual *I* produced, to make it into a resource that *you* have contributed to and enhanced by way of your note-taking – a joint project.

Having reached this end point of the manual, I hope that you will not see it as the end point of your learning but, rather, I hope that what we have worked on will have inspired you to go on thinking about the issues that matter. I hope too that it has given you food for thought about the part you can play in challenging the ageist assumption that it is acceptable to treat people differently, and less fairly, just because they are old. We are all people, regardless of whether we are the people providing the care and support, or receiving the care and support.

Old age is not something 'out there' and disconnected from our lives. Unless we die young, then it will be part of our own life experience. Every day we're alive we're all getting further down the road on our own journey through life. The renowned author, C. S. Lewis, is credited with saying 'You are never too old to set a new goal or to dream a new dream'. It disheartens me when I hear of obstacles being put in the way of some older people's goals or dreams being realised, even though that might be unintentional.

In the conclusion to their book *Age and Dignity*, Thompson and Cox (2024) offer some very useful guidelines for eldercare practitioners but make the point that such guidelines on their own are not enough to guarantee dignified eldercare:

> No list of practical guidelines can ensure anti-ageist practice. A commitment to promoting dignity for older people entails a commitment to recognizing, challenging and undermining ageism. Practical guidelines can assist or facilitate putting this commitment into practice, but what they cannot do is act as a substitute for such commitment ... They are, then, part of the solution, but they are not sufficient in themselves to guarantee that work with older people is characterized by dignity and is free from negative stereotypes. We can, however, draw strength from the fact that, by striving towards anti-ageist practice, we are making a contribution towards a positive experience of old age, one characterized by dignity, not alienation; empowerment not discrimination, inclusion, not marginalization.
>
> *(p. 215)*

It is for that reason that I have chosen to add a subtitle to this second edition – A *Values* Perspective – to stress the relationship between values and actions because our commitment to particular values is what drives us to act in particular ways and for particular reasons.

It is to be hoped that the thinking spaces that this manual has provided will have further developed your appreciation of the right of *every* older person, whatever difficulties have led to your being called on to support them, to have their goals and dreams recognised as such. I know that I'll reach the end of my journey as the unique person *I* consider myself to be, and my hope is that other people will know that person or make it their business to find out. It is a hope I have for all older people who find themselves in need of support to live their lives on their terms, and we owe it to our future selves. Thank you for joining me in this enterprise.

Guide to further learning

Suggestions for further reading

Applewhite, A. (2019) *This Chair Rocks: A Manifesto Against Ageism*, Celadon Books.

Bernard, M., Ray, M. and Reynolds, J. (2020) *The Evolution of British Gerontology: Personal Perspectives and Historical Developments*, Policy Press.

Bruce, S. (2018) *Sociology: A Very Short Introduction*, Oxford University Press.

Gawande, A. (2015) *Being Mortal: Illness, Medicine and What Happens in the End*, Profile Books.

Giddens, A. and Sutton, P. W. (2021) *Sociology*, 9e, Polity.

Goldman, C. (2018) *Wisdom from Those in Care: Conversations, Insights and Inspiration*, The Society of Certified Senior Advisors.

Gutterman, A. S. (2023) *Ageism and Ableism*, Older People's Rights Project.

Kartupelis, J. (2020) *Making Relational Care Work for Older People: Exploring Innovation and Best Practice in Everyday Life*, Routledge.

Kottler, J. A. (2020) *Practicing What You Preach: Self-care for Helping Professionals*, Cognella Academic Publishing.

Lee, S., Fenge, L-A., Brown, K. and Lyne, M. (eds) (2020) *Demystifying Mental Capacity: A Guide for Health and Social Care Professionals*, Learning Matters.

Leland, J. (2018) *Happiness Is a Choice You Make: Lessons from a Year Amongst the Oldest Old*, Farrar, Strauss and Giroux.

Leonardo, N. (2020) *Active Listening Techniques: 30 Practical Tools to Hone Your Communication Skills*, Calisto.

Lustbader, W. (1991) *Counting on Kindness: The Dilemmas of Dependency*, The Free Press.

McCormack, B., McCance, T., Bully, C., Brown, D., McMillan, A. and Martin, S. (eds) (2021) *Fundamentals of Person-centred Healthcare Practice*, Wiley-Blackwell.

Minkler, M. and Estes, C. (eds) (1999) *Critical Gerontology: Perspectives from Political and Moral Economy*, Baywood Publishing.

Moss, B. and Thompson, N. (2020) *The Values-based Practice Manual*, Avenue Media Solutions.

Nelson, T. D. (ed.) (2017) *Ageism: Stereotyping and Prejudice Against Older Persons*, 2e, MIT Press.

Patmore. C. and McNulty, A. (2017) *Caring for the Whole Person: Home Care Which Promotes Well-being and Choice*, The Well-Being and Choice in Services for Older People Project.

Pooley, C. (2024) *How to Age Dis-Gracefully*, Penguin.

Rogers, C. R. and Farson, R. E. (2015) *Active Listening*, Marlino Publishing.

Salt, T. (2021) *Towards Outstanding: A Guide to Excellence in Health and Social Care*, Luminate.

Sanderson, H., Bown, H. and Bailey, G. (2015) *Person-centred Thinking with Older People: 6 Essential Practices*, Jessica Kingsley Publishers.

Stone, D. (2019) *The Essential Family Guide to Caring for Older People*, Green Tree.

Sasser, J. (2018) *Gerontology: The Basics*, Taylor and Francis.

Tanner, D. (2010) *Managing the Ageing Experience: Learning from Older People*, Policy Press.

Tanner, D. (2020) 'Resilience and older people', in N. Thompson and G. R. Cox (eds) (2020) *Promoting Resilience: Responding to Adversity, Vulnerability and Loss*, Routledge.

Thompson, N. (2017) *Theorizing Practice*, 2nd edn. Bloomsbury.

Thompson, N. (2021) *Anti-Discriminatory Practice: Equality, Diversity and Social Justice*, 7th edn, Bloomsbury.

Thompson, N. and Cox, G. R. (eds) (2017) *Handbook of the Sociology of Death, Grief and Bereavement: A Guide to Theory and Practice*, Routledge.

Thompson, N. and Cox, G. R. (eds) (2020) *Promoting Resilience: Responding to Adversity, Vulnerability and Loss*, Routledge.

Thompson, N. and Cox G. R. (2024) *Age and Dignity: Anti-Ageist Theory and Practice*, Edward Elgar.

Thompson, S. and Thompson, N. (2023) *The Critically Reflective Practitioner*, 3rd edn, Bloomsbury.

UNPRD (UN Partnership on the Rights of Persons with Disabilities) and UN Women (no date) *Intersectionality Resource Guide and Toolkit: An Intersectional Approach to Leave No One Behind*, UN Women

Websites you might find helpful
(correct at time of writing)
agedcarecrisis.com
alzheimers.org.uk
info@ageing-better.org.uk
cpa.org.uk/
centreformentalhealth.org.uk/making-mental-health-services-work-for-older-people/
mha.org.uk
thecareworkerscharity.org.uk/
www.unison.org.uk/care-workers-your-rights/

References

Age UK ageuk.org.uk

Benatar, S. (2016) 'Living, suffering, and dying', in D. L. Harris and T. C. Bordere (eds) (2016) *Handbook of Social Justice in Loss and Grief: Exploring Diversity, Equity, and Inclusion*, Routledge.

Borgstrom, E. and Visser, R. (2025) *Critical Approaches to Death, Dying and Bereavement*, Routledge.

Butler, R. N. (1963) 'The life review: An interpretation of reminiscence in the aged', *Human Development*, 16(1): 24–33.

Crossley, N. (1996) *Intersubjectivity: The Fabric of Social Becoming*, Sage.

Harris, D. L. and Bordere, T. C. (eds) (2016) *Handbook of Social Justice in Loss and Grief: Exploring Diversity, Equity, and Inclusion*, Routledge.

Kaiser, P. and Eley, R. (eds) (2016) *Life Story Work with People with Dementia: Ordinary Lives, Extraordinary People*, Jessica Kingsley.

Klass, D., Silverman, P. R. and Nickman, S. (eds) (1996) *Continuing Bonds: New Understandings of Grief*, Routledge.

Livingston, W., Redcliffe, J. and Aziz, H. Q. (2023) *Social Work in Wales*, Polity.

Lustbader, W. (1991) *Counting on Kindness: The Dilemmas of Dependency*, The Free Press.

Midwinter, E. (1990) 'An ageing world: The equivocal response', *Ageing and Society*, 10(2): 221–228.

Neimeyer, R. A. and Sands, D. C. (2011) 'Meaning reconstruction in bereavement: from principles to practice', in R. A. Neimeyer, D. L. Harris, H. R. Winouker and G. F. Thornton (2011) *Grief and Bereavement in Contemporary Society: Bridging Research and Practice*, Routledge.

Neimeyer, R. A., Harris, D. L., Winouker, H. R. and Thornton, G. F. (eds) (2011) *Grief and Bereavement in Contemporary Society: Bridging Research and Practice*, Routledge.

Office for National Statistics (ONS) www.ons.gov.uk

Papadatou, D. (2009) *In the Face of Death: Professionals who Care for the Dying and the Bereaved*, Springer.

Robinson, J. L. and Hawranik, P. (2000) 'Reminiscence therapy with older adults: A meta-analysis', *Aging and Mental Health*, 4(3): 178–192.

Swift, H. and Chasteen, A. (2021) 'Ageism in the time of Covid-19', *Group Processes & Intergroup Relations*, 24(2): 246–252.

Tanner, D. (2010) *Managing the Ageing Experience: Learning from Older People*, Policy Press.

Thompson, N. (2017) *Theorizing Practice*, 2nd edn, Palgrave.

Thompson, N. (2021) *Anti-Discriminatory Practice: Equality, Diversity and Social Justice*, 7th edn, Bloomsbury.

Thompson, N. (2022) *The Loss and Grief Practice Manual*, Wrexham, Avenue Media Solutions.

Thompson, N. and Cox, G. R. (eds) (2020) *Promoting Resilience: Responding to Adversity, Vulnerability, and Loss*, Abingdon, Routledge.

Thompson, N. and Cox, G. R. (2024) *Age and Dignity: Anti-Ageist Theory and Practice*, Edward Elgar.

Waters, S-J. (2023) 'Coproduction and service user involvement', in W. Livingston, J. Redcliffe and H. Q. Aziz (2023) *Social Work in Wales*, Polity.

Yalom, I. D. (2008) *Staring at the Sun: Overcoming the Dread of Death*, Piatkus.

Also by Sue Thompson

Books

Age Discrimination (Russell House Publishing, 2005)
Reciprocity and Dependency in Old Age: Indian and UK Perspectives (Springer, 2013)
The Social Work Companion (with Thompson, N., 2nd edn, Palgrave, 2015)
The Critically Reflective Practitioner (with Thompson, N., 3rd edn, Bloomsbury)

E-books

Don't Be Your Own Worst Enemy: Self-care for Busy People (Avenue Media Solutions, 2012)
Job Interviews: Giving yourself the best chance (Avenue Media Solutions, 2012)
Procrastination: Putting things off and how to stop doing it (Avenue Media Solutions, 2012)
Active Listening: How to communicate better (with R. Wallace, Avenue Media Solutions, 2013)

Index

Note: *Italic* page numbers indicate figures.

For Product Safety Concerns and Information please contact our EU
representative GPSR@taylorandfrancis.com
Taylor & Francis Verlag GmbH, Kaufingerstraße 24, 80331 München, Germany

www.ingramcontent.com/pod-product-compliance
Lightning Source LLC
Chambersburg PA
CBHW070351270326
41926CB00017B/4082